Conduct Unbecoming

A Play in Three Acts

by Barry England

A SAMUEL FRENCH ACTING EDITION

New York Hollywood London Toronto
SAMUELFRENCH.COM

Copyright © 1971 by Barry England

ALL RIGHTS RESERVED

CAUTION: Professionals and amateurs are hereby warned that *CONDUCT UNBECOMING* is subject to a Licensing Fee. It is fully protected under the copyright laws of the United States of America, the British Commonwealth, including Canada, and all other countries of the Copyright Union. All rights, including professional, amateur, motion picture, recitation, lecturing, public reading, radio broadcasting, television and the rights of translation into foreign languages are strictly reserved. In its present form the play is dedicated to the reading public only.

The amateur live stage performance rights to *CONDUCT UNBECOMING* are controlled exclusively by Samuel French, Inc., and licensing arrangements and performance licenses must be secured well in advance of presentation. PLEASE NOTE that amateur Licensing Fees are set upon application in accordance with your producing circumstances. When applying for a licensing quotation and a performance license please give us the number of performances intended, dates of production, your seating capacity and admission fee. Licensing Fees are payable one week before the opening performance of the play to Samuel French, Inc., at 45 W. 25th Street, New York, NY 10010.

Licensing Fee of the required amount must be paid whether the play is presented for charity or gain and whether or not admission is charged.

Stock licensing fees quoted upon application to Samuel French, Inc.

For all other rights than those stipulated above, apply to: Samuel French, Inc.

Particular emphasis is laid on the question of amateur or professional readings, permission and terms for which must be secured in writing from Samuel French, Inc.

Copying from this book in whole or in part is strictly forbidden by law, and the right of performance is not transferable.

Whenever the play is produced the following notice must appear on all programs, printing and advertising for the play: "Produced by special arrangement with Samuel French, Inc."

Due authorship credit must be given on all programs, printing and advertising for the play.

No one shall commit or authorize any act or omission by which the copyright of, or the right to copyright, this play may be impaired.
No one shall make any changes in this play for the purpose of production.
Publication of this play does not imply availability for performance. Both amateurs and professionals considering a production are strongly advised in their own interests to apply to Samuel French, Inc., for written permission before starting rehearsals, advertising, or booking a theatre.
No part of this book may be reproduced, stored in a retrieval system, or transmitted in any form, by any means, now known or yet to be invented, including mechanical, electronic, photocopying, recording, videotaping, or otherwise, without the prior written permission of the publisher.

ISBN 978-0-573-60723-3   Printed in U.S.A.   #5133

CONDUCT UNBECOMING was first presented by Donald Albery and Roger L. Stevens at the Ethel Barrymore Theatre, N.Y.C., in October 1970. The director was Val May. The original cast was as follows:

CAST

2ND LT. EDWARD MILLINGTON .... *Jeremy Clyde*
2ND LT. ARTHUR DRAKE .... *Paul Jones*
THE COLONEL, COLONEL STRANG .. *Michael Barrington*
MAJOR LIONEL ROACH .... *Michael Bradshaw*
   The Second in Command
MAJOR ALASTAIR WIMBOURNE, V.C. ..... *Paul Harding*
LT.-COL. MAURICE PRATT .... *Robert Hewitt*
   The Doctor
CAPT. RUPERT HARPER .... *Donald Pickering*
   The Adjutant
LT. RICHARD FOTHERGILL .... *Richard Lupino*
   Senior Subaltern
LT. FRANK HART .... *Richard Clarke*
2ND LT. JOHN TRULY .... *Nicholas Hammond*
2ND LT. SIMON BOULTON .... *Robert Murch*
2ND LT. EDWARD WINTERS .... *Noel Craig*
2ND LT. FRANK HUTTON .... *Edwin Owens*
PRADAH SINGH .... *Ronald Drake*
   The Mess Major Domo
MESS HEAD WAITER .... *Thomas Cover*
MRS. MARJORIE HASSELTINE ...... *Elizabeth Shepherd*

MEM STRANG .... *Sylvia O'Brien*
   The Colonel's Wife
MRS. BANDANAI .... *Madhur Jaffrey*
LAL .... *Pandora Bronson Lupino*
   An Indian Servant Woman
LADIES AT THE BALL .... *Vanya Franck,
              Pandora Bronson Lupino, Jean Hogan*
WAITERS .... *James Tripp, Carl Jessop,
                                       James Leggi*

India—1882

The Ante-room to a British Army Officers' Mess

CHARACTERS

2ND LT. EDWARD MILLINGTON
2ND LT. ARTHUR DRAKE
COLONEL STRANG, *the Colonel*
MAJOR LIONEL ROACH, *the Second in Command*
MAJOR ALASTAIR WIMBORNE, V. C.
LT. COL. MAURICE PRATT, *the Doctor*
CAPT. RUPERT HARPER, *the Adjutant*
2ND LT. RICHARD FOTHERGILL, *the Senior Subaltern*
LT. FRANK HART
2ND LT. JOHN TRULY
2ND LT. SIMON BOULTON
2ND LT. EDWARD WINTERS
2ND LT. FRANK HUTTON
PRADAH SINGH, *the Mess Major Domo*

MRS. MARJORIE HASSELTINE, *a Widow*
MEM STRANG, *the Colonel's Lady*
MRS. BANDANAI, *a Widow*
LAL, *an Indian Servant Woman*

INDIAN MESS WAITERS (4)
FEMALE GUESTS (3)

TIME AND PLACE: India in the late Eighteen Hundreds

Conduct Unbecoming

ACT ONE

SCENE 1

The mess. (The anteroom.) Afternoon. DRAKE *enters, double doors* R. *followed by* MILLINGTON. DRAKE *looks about him as a man finally at peace.* MILLINGTON, *with gloom. A silence.*

DRAKE. (*Crosses* D. *to* R. C. *Looks with reverence.*) Exactly as I imagined it would be.
MILLINGTON. (*Crosses* D. R. *of* DRAKE.) How *very* uplifting for you.
DRAKE. (*Crosses* L. *Looks out arch.*) I should hardly expect you to understand.
MILLINGTON. But I do, my dear fellow. You forget. This place has haunted my childhood, too.
DRAKE. You appear to have learned little enough respect for it.
MILLINGTON. I've a very *healthy* respect for it. One should always fear ghosts.

(DRAKE *stares at Regimental mementoes.*)

DRAKE. (*Breaks* D. *Quietly.*) It is like . . . coming home.
MILLINGTON. Isn't it, though? (*Notices, crosses* R. *to one of the portraits.*) Good heavens. The Old Fellow himself.
DRAKE. (*Turns, crosses* L. *of* R. *coffee table, puts hat down.*) Your father?

8　　　　CONDUCT UNBECOMING　　　ACT I

MILLINGTON. (*Drifts* U. *and* L. *of* DRAKE. *Drily:*) Doesn't he look splendid?

DRAKE. (*Crosses* R. *to read plaque. Reads:*) "General Sir William Millington, V.C. Colonel of the Regiment, 1875–1881."

MILLINGTON. (*Turns away.*) Not to mention Order of the Bath. (L. *of* R. *coffee table. Makes it sound absurd.*) Sheriff of the County, Justice of the Peace . . .

DRAKE. (*Turns to him.*) You will find only military honours here. These are past colonels and holders of the Victoria Cross. That is the Regimental tradition.

MILLINGTON. (*Crosses* L. C.) *Ah.*

DRAKE. (*Inspects medals* R.) As a general's son, you will be expected to know these things. (*A silence.*)

MILLINGTON. (*Charming smile.*) I can always turn to you for information, can't I? (*Slight pause.*)

DRAKE. You will find no portrait of my father here. He was a major.

MILLINGTON. But, my dear fellow, "Backbone of the Mess." How often have I heard the general say . . .

DRAKE. (*Breaks* U. R. *abruptly.*) We should present ourselves to the adjutant.

MILLINGTON. (*Checks decanter* D. L.) If we can find him. Or indeed anyone.

DRAKE. (*Hesitates* R.) Yes, I . . . don't quite understand where everyone can be.

MILLINGTON. (*Turns to* D. R.) You don't suppose there's been another *Mutiny?* (*A silence.*)

DRAKE. (*Crosses* L. *to* L. C. *table.*) I think I should warn you, Millington, that while I might—through force of circumstance—tolerate your imbecilities throughout our voyage together, you will find they are not appreciated here.

MILLINGTON. (*Holding bottle.*) Oh, but my dear fellow, we are not yet officially members of the Regiment. Won't you allow me a moment or two more of my native *joie de vivre?* (*Sniffs contents.*)

DRAKE. You realize, of course, that how you choose to behave will reflect on me?

MILLINGTON. Surely not?

DRAKE. There is no question of it. Unfortunately, we shall be judged together. (MILLINGTON *replaces bottle.*)

MILLINGTON. (*Turns to* D. R.) Oh, dear . . .

DRAKE. (*At* L. C. *table.*) I should therefore tell you that I have every intention of making a success of my three months' probationary period with this Regiment, and joining it properly and fully at the end of that time. (*Crosses to* R. C. *table, picks up hat.*)

MILLINGTON. That is kind of you, Arthur. Thank you. There is, unhappily, a little matter I should *perhaps* share with *you*.

DRAKE. What is that?

MILLINGTON. (*Breaks* L. *Very emphatic.*) I have *no* intention *whatsoever* of surviving my three months' probationary period. There is a ship, (*Crosses to* D. L. C. *chair.*) the *Doric Castle*, which sails for England in almost exactly three months to the day from now. I intend to be on her. (*Sits.*)

(*Before* DRAKE *can react*, PRADAH SINGH *enters* C. *of veranda [from off* R.]. *Crosses* D. L. C. *Stately, dignified, sixties. He bows.*)

PRADAH. Good afternoon, gentlemen. May I be of service?

DRAKE. . . . You must be Pradah Singh.

PRADAH. And you are Mister Drake. If I may say, you are most like your father, under whom I had the honour to serve.

DRAKE. Thank you.

PRADAH. (*Turns to him.*) I also had the honour to serve under your father, Millington sahib. Though I was, of course, younger then, a mere boy.

MILLINGTON. Yes, he did have me rather late in the day.

PRADAH. (*Taken aback.*) . . . He was a fine gentleman, sahib.

MILLINGTON. So I am always being told.

DRAKE. (*Rescues* PRADAH SINGH. *A step to* C.) I believe your father served also with the Regiment, Pradah Singh.

PRADAH. My grandfather, also, sahib. (*Watching* MILLINGTON.) In my family it is the tradition.

MILLINGTON. (*Rises, crosses to* PRADAH. *Clicks fingers.*) Pradah Singh, I fancy I could do great service to a large whiskey and soda. I wonder if you would be so kind as to . . .

DRAKE. That's quite out of the question.

MILLINGTON. In heaven's name, why?

DRAKE. We may neither order nor accept drinks until we are properly introduced into the Mess.

MILLINGTON. (*Breaks* D. *a step.*) Good God.

PRADAH. I am sorry, sahib. I regret that is . . .

MILLINGTON. (*Crossing* R. *below, sits* D. R. C. *table.*) The tradition. Just so. Well, heaven send we be introduced soon. (PRADAH *crosses* L., *inspects drinks.*)

DRAKE. Quite. Pradah Singh, we seem unable to locate the Adjutant. Or indeed . . .

PRADAH. (*Turns to* DRAKE.) It is the polo, sahib. The end of season match against the Seventh Lancers.

DRAKE. (*Crosses* U. C. *a step.*) Blast! Of course! I should have remembered!

PRADAH. (*Picks up* D. L. *chair.*) The Colonel will be leading in the ladies soon.

MILLINGTON. Voluptuous ladies?

DRAKE. (PRADAH *places chair* D. L. *of* L. C. *table.* DRAKE *crosses* R. *to* MILLINGTON.) For God's sake, man!

(*The* SENIOR SUBALTERN *bustles in* R. *double doors.*)

SENIOR SUBALTERN. (*Crosses to* R. *of* PRADAH.) Ah, there you are! Pradah Singh! A vast, rapid stengah! (*Crosses to* L. C. *table.*) We've about two minutes in hand! (PRADAH *turns to booze* D. L.)

PRADAH. Sahib.

SENIOR SUBALTERN. (*Turns to them.*) What about you chaps?

MILLINGTON. Oh, my dear fellow. Just anything. (FOTHERGILL *stiffens.*) I am about to expire.

DRAKE. My companion is joking, of course. We're fully aware of the Regimental tradition.

SENIOR SUBALTERN. (*Relaxes.*) Good. Splendid. Well done. (*Turns to him.*) Thank you, Pradah Singh. (PRADAH SINGH *puts down bottle. Withdraws* L. *arch.*) Damned silly, these little tests. But one must be certain.

MILLINGTON. (*Steps* R.) Oh, no. . . .

SENIOR SUBALTERN. (*Crosses* R. *to* DRAKE. *Extends hand to* DRAKE.) You must be Millington.

DRAKE. (*In confusion.*) Er, no, no. . . .

MILLINGTON. I have that dubious honour, my dear fellow.

SENIOR SUBALTERN. Oh. Sorry. (*Crosses to* MILLINGTON. *They shake hands.*) I'm Fothergill, Senior Subaltern. You're Drake, then.

DRAKE. Yes. (*They shake hands.*)

SENIOR SUBALTERN. Good. Well. Sit down, chaps. Lot to tell you, devil of a little time to tell it in. (DRAKE *crosses to chair* L. *of* R. C. *table.* SENIOR SUBALTERN *perches arm of chair.*)

MILLINGTON. We are allowed to sit?

SENIOR SUBALTERN. Of course. Why not?

MILLINGTON. I just thought it might be another of those little tests. Pay no attention, please. (*Sinks deep into* COLONEL'S *chair* R. *of* R. C. *table.* FOTHERGILL *steps above table, looking at* D. R.)

DRAKE. Mister Millington has a very personal sense of humour.

SENIOR SUBALTERN. (*Looks at* MILLINGTON.) Oh. Yes, of course—very funny. Ah, ha. You're sitting in the Colonel's chair, old man. (*It is a moment before it dawns on* MILLINGTON *that he is the guilty party. He springs up, breaks* D. R.)

MILLINGTON. Oh, great heavens! I shouldn't want to add sacrilege to my other crimes. Now should I? (*Crosses to* D. R. *chair*.)

SENIOR SUBALTERN. No. Quite. Now, I'm Fothergill, as I say, and it's my . . . (DRAKE *sits* L. C. *chair*. MILLINGTON, *having backed to another chair* D. R., *is peering over his shoulder at it, hovering.* L. *of* MILLINGTON, D.) Is there something wrong, old man?

MILLINGTON. This . . . . isn't . . . ?

SENIOR SUBALTERN. No. No, it isn't.

MILLINGTON. No. Good. (*Sits,* D. R. *chair, smiles at* DRAKE.) One is anxious to do the proper thing.

SENIOR SUBALTERN. Quite. (*Strikes boot with stick*.) Now then. It's my job as Senior Subaltern to watch over you chaps for the next week or two. Make sure you understand what's what and so on. (*Sits* R. *arm of* R. C. *chair*.) So let me remind you of one or two of the basic facts of life. You don't *speak* to anyone, of course. Nor will anyone speak to you. Except me. It's my job to speak to you. And you may speak to me. But never to a senior officer—unless addressed first—in which case, you reply, "Yes, sir." (*Comes to attention*.) Unless it is the Colonel, in which case you reply, "Yes, Colonel." We always (*Sits*.) call the Colonel, Colonel, in this regiment.

DRAKE. Quite.

SENIOR SUBALTERN. Quite.

MILLINGTON. That seems an eminently sound arrangement.

SENIOR SUBALTERN. (*Crosses* D. R. *to* MILLINGTON—*level*.) Yes, quite, quite. (*Rises*.) Now then. When the Colonel arrives in a few moments with the ladies and the other officers . . .

MILLINGTON. Forgive me, my dear fellow, I have a query.

SENIOR SUBALTERN. Well?

MILLINGTON. If we are not to speak, how are we to make our intentions known?

SENIOR SUBALTERN. Junior officers do not have intentions.

MILLINGTON. Well . . . Suppose we should wish to—er—leave the room?

SENIOR SUBALTERN. I should try using the door, my dear fellow. But never before the Colonel, of course.

MILLINGTON. I do hope his bladder is weaker than mine.

SENIOR SUBALTERN. (*Threatening pace to him.*) I think you will find this whole operation will go a great deal more smoothly, Millington, if you remain silent. I should add that silence is a quality much admired in junior officers.

MILLINGTON. My dear fellow, I shan't utter another word.

SENIOR SUBALTERN. (*Crosses L. to arch.*) Good. Excellent. Now, when the Colonel arrives, we shall withdraw to a corner over there. At an appropriate moment, I shall strike the gong, (*Demonstrates.*) announce Strangers in the Mess, and introduce each of you individually. No one will pay the least attention except the Colonel, who will say, "Thank you, Mister Fothergill." You will say nothing. (*Crosses U. R. of R. C. chair.*) We shall then wait for the Adjutant to join us, when you will present yourselves, and we shall withdraw to your quarters. Now, as to the ladies . . . In the Colonel's party this afternoon there will be, I think, only Mem Strang herself, the Colonel's lady, and, ah . . . Mrs. Hasseltine. (*Glances nervously about. He is plainly embarrassed.*)

DRAKE. The widow of Major Hasseltine.

SENIOR SUBALTERN. (*Sits R. arm of R. C. chair.*) Yes. Yes. I, ah . . . should perhaps say a word or two about Mrs. Hasseltine. (*Silence. He labours on.*) She is a lady —much admired in the Mess. Very popular. A—regular feature of our lives here. However. She is not above—returning certain favours—particularly to (MILLINGTON *reacts.*) younger officers. (*Turns to* MILLINGTON, *points crop*.) Don't misunderstand me. She is very much a lady, but . . .

DRAKE. Yes. Of course. Most distressing.

(MILLINGTON *is now fully attentive*.)

SENIOR SUBALTERN. Yes. Quite. My point is, junior officers are well advised to remain—unsusceptible. (*Crosses* L. *above Drake's chair*.) She is a very attractive woman. However, certain senior officers having—you understand me?—"made a point" with Mrs. Hasseltine . . .

DRAKE. (*Shocked, disapproving*.) Oh. I see.

SENIOR SUBALTERN. (*Rises, crosses* D. R. *a step*.) Of course, this is a matter of which, while you should be fully apprised, you know nothing.

DRAKE. No, quite. (*Rises*.)

SENIOR SUBALTERN. Just remain—courteous, but . . .

MILLINGTON. (*Rises*.) Distant?

SENIOR SUBALTERN. Distant, (*Turns to him*.) yes.

DRAKE. Enough is said. (*Turns* U. L. *of* L. C. *chair*.)

SENIOR SUBALTERN. Good. (*Goes up to see if* COLONEL *is coming yet with his party. Crosses* U. *onto veranda* C.) Yes, well, I don't know if you've any other questions?

MILLINGTON. (*Crosses* U. *to showcase*.) As a matter of fact, my dear fellow . . .

SENIOR SUBALTERN. Yes?

MILLINGTON. I was wondering what on earth this filthy, scruffy old tunic can possibly be doing in the Mess? (*Immediate outrage from the* OTHERS. *This is a calculated provocation*.)

SENIOR SUBALTERN. (*Steps to him*.) Mr. Millington . . .

DRAKE. (*Steps in* L. *of* FOTHERGILL.) You know perfectly well, Millington!

SENIOR SUBALTERN. That was Captain Scarlett's tunic! He was wearing it at the battle of Ratjahpur!

MILLINGTON. (*Turns to* R. C. *chair*.) It must have been a very messy affair.

ACT I   CONDUCT UNBECOMING   15

SENIOR SUBALTERN. (*Advancing.*) Warfare is not noted for its comfort, Mister Millington. Nor is the future of young officers who fail to acquaint themselves with the history and traditions of this Regiment! You hear me? (*Stamps foot, crosses to* MILLINGTON, *who snaps to attention.*) You will memorise and recite to me the known facts of the death of Captain Scarlett, who is a hero of this Regiment and will be honoured as such by you!

(*Silence.* MILLINGTON *looks again at tunic.*)

MILLINGTON. Still, when you come to think of it, it must smell absolutely frightful.
SENIOR SUBALTERN. Mister Millington!

(SENIOR SUBALTERN *raises cane, almost as though he might strike* MILLINGTON. PRADAH SINGH *enters, followed by* MESS WAITERS.)

PRADAH. The Colonel is just arriving, sahib, with the ladies.
SENIOR SUBALTERN. Thank you, Pradah Singh. (*Turns away.*) Over here. (*Goes to* D. L. *table. As they follow,* DRAKE *snarls at* MILLINGTON.)
DRAKE. Pull yourself together, man!
MILLINGTON. But, my dear f—
DRAKE. I am being judged, too!

(*The* COLONEL *enters* R. *door with* MRS. MARJORIE HASSELTINE, MEM STRANG [R. *of* COLONEL], MAJOR WIMBORNE, V.C. [*who is in polo gear with scarf*], *the* DOCTOR, *the* SECOND IN COMMAND, *the* ADJUTANT [*also in polo gear*], LT. HART [*in polo gear*], 2ND LTS. WINTERS, BOULTON *and* HUTTON.)

MRS. HASSELTINE. (*Over shoulder, crosses to* L. C. *chair.*) I'm sure you are wrong, Colonel. I'll wager it is seven, not six. What do you say, Mem?

MEM. Oh, dear. I'm not very good at that sort of thing, I'm afraid. I'd have to look it up. (*All in places.*)

COLONEL. (WIMBORNE *enters* R. *doors—to* BOULTON:) Lionel will know. Tell us, Lionel. How many matches are we up on the Lancers now?

ROACH. Seven, Colonel, counting today's.

MRS. HASSELTINE. (*Crosses* D. L. C.) There you are. What did I say?

WIMBORNE. (*Crosses* D. R. *to medal cabinet. Puts down mallet and helmet.*) We really will have to scratch that fixture soon, Colonel. (*Chuckles.*)

COLONEL. Oh, I don't think tradition is ever pointless, is it, Alastair?

WIMBORNE. (*Grins, turns to* COLONEL.) No, no, perhaps not.

DOCTOR. (*Crosses* D. *to* L. *of* WIMBORNE.) Besides, you enjoy whacking (*Laughs.*) the pants off them, Alastair. You know damned well you do.

WIMBORNE. How right you are, Doctor.

MRS. HASSELTINE. (*Crosses* R. *to* WIMBORNE.) He's a clever boy, isn't he, Colonel, to have scored two such beautiful goals?

WIMBORNE. (*A step to her, kisses her hand.*) My dear Marge, I did it all for you! (*Reactions.*)

COLONEL. (*Crosses* U. *to* WINTERS GROUP U. R. C. MRS. HASSELTINE *talks to* DOCTOR.) He left it damned late in the day, I will say. We'll go straight out onto the veranda, Pradah Singh. (*Crosses* D. C.)

PRADAH. Very good, Colonel.

COLONEL. Marjorie, my dear. (*She crosses* L. *to him.* MEM *and* ROACH *cross* D. *to* DOCTOR *around* R. C. *table.*)

(PRADAH SINGH *taps hands,* WAITERS *run out to veranda.* COLONEL *indicates* MRS. HASSELTINE *to precede him.* SENIOR SUBALTERN *seizes chance to tap gong. All continue talking—*COLONEL *turns to* FOTHERGILL.)

SENIOR SUBALTERN. (*At attention.*) Colonel. There are

Strangers in the Mess, Colonel. May I present Mister Millington. And Mister Drake, Colonel.

(*The* COLONEL *looks at them a moment.*)

COLONEL. (*After brief look at new men* COLONEL *turns to* MRS. HASSELTINE *and offers arm.*) Thank you, Mister Fothergill. (*Turns to leave with his party.* MRS. HASSELTINE *is looking at* MILLINGTON. *To* MRS. HASSELTINE.) As I was saying . . .

MRS. HASSELTINE. (*She holds back to look.*) Surely that is never William Millington's boy? (*They move* U. *to level with* L. C. *table. Glances back.*) He looks far too young. (*The* COLONEL, *embarrassed, is about to reply when* MILLINGTON *speaks.*)

MILLINGTON. With respect, ma'am, (*Silence from all,* COLONEL *and* MRS. HASSELTINE *look at* MILLINGTON.) I hardly believe you can have known my father. You also look far too young. (ADJUTANT, BOULTON *and* HART *make slight break on stage.* WINTERS, HUTTON, WIMBORNE *break* D. *for a look. A shocked, cold silence.* MEM *intervenes.*)

MEM. (*Crosses to* MRS. HASSELTINE.) Shall we, my dear . . . ?

MRS. HASSELTINE. (*Amused. She and* MEM *exit veranda* L.) By your leave, Mister Millington. (WIMBORNE *crosses* D. *a step, looks at* MILLINGTON.)

MEM. (COLONEL *steps* D., *looking first at* FOTHERGILL *then* MILLINGTON *as:*) Tell me, how are you getting along with that new gel of yours? What is her name? I will keep forgetting their names. . . . (*They are now off. A pause. The* COLONEL *follows, the others taking their cue from him.*)

COLONEL. (*Turns to* DOCTOR.) How is young Truly, Doctor?

DOCTOR. (*Crosses to* COLONEL, *exits veranda* L. [*Both*].) Not too badly, thank you, Colonel. Be up and about in a day or two.

WIMBORNE. (*Follows, looking at* MILLINGTON, *exits veranda* R.) Took a nasty knock, you know. Played a damned fine game, though. Put that vital pass through to me in the last minutes. . . .

(*They are off.* WINTERS *and* HUTTON *follow—veranda* R. *Then* ROACH, *who looks back at* ADJUTANT *on steps as he reaches veranda, exits* L. PRADAH *follows. The* SECOND IN COMMAND, *last to leave, looks at* MILLINGTON, *at the* ADJUTANT, *frowns, departs. There remain only* ADJUTANT, *stiff with anger,* SENIOR SUBALTERN, DRAKE *and* MILLINGTON. *A silence.*)

ADJUTANT. (*Crosses* L. *to* C.) Well, Mister Fothergill?
SENIOR SUBALTERN. (*Steps forward informally.*) I'm sorry, Mister Har- . . .
ADJUTANT. I did not hear that, Mister Fothergill.
SENIOR SUBALTERN. (*Jumps to attention.*) . . . I must have failed to make my instructions plain.
ADJUTANT. You are assumed to be capable of the duties of your office, Mister Fothergill. That is why you hold it.
SENIOR SUBALTERN. Yes, Mister Harper. (*A silence.*)
ADJUTANT. (*Crosses* D. R. *to medal case.*) I am waiting, Mister Fothergill.
SENIOR SUBALTERN. (*Hisses at* DRAKE.) Present yourself, man!
DRAKE. (*Smart pace forward to attention.*) I have the honour to present myself, sir. Mister Drake, sir.
ADJUTANT. (*Crosses to* D. R. *of* R. C. *table. Looks him up and down.*) . . . Thank you, Mister Drake.
MILLINGTON. (*One pace forward to attention.*) I, also, have the honour to present myself, sir.
ADJUTANT. Do you lack a name, sir?
MILLINGTON. Millington, sir. (*A silence.*)
ADJUTANT. Come here, Mister Millington.
MILLINGTON. Sir. (*In silence* MILLINGTON, *subdued by*

this cutting, cold, quiet man, goes to stand before him. Marches to D. L. *of* R. C. *table. At attention. A pause.*)

ADJUTANT. If I hear from you again, it will be for the last time. Do you understand me?

MILLINGTON. May I be allowed to say . . .

ADJUTANT. Be quiet! (*A cracked whip. A pause.*) Now. Have I made myself quite plain?

MILLINGTON. Yes, sir.

ADJUTANT. Return to your place. (MILLINGTON *does so. Turns in line with* DRAKE. *Silence.*) If you find your duties too arduous, Mister Fothergill, I can arrange to have you relieved of them.

SENIOR SUBALTERN. . . . No, sir.

ADJUTANT. That is all. (*He goes, veranda* R.)

SENIOR SUBALTERN. (*Rounds on* MILLINGTON.) You bloody little fool! What the hell were you playing at?!

MILLINGTON. I'm sorry, my dear fellow . . .

SENIOR SUBALTERN. Be quiet! I told you to remain silent while there were senior officers in the Mess!

MILLINGTON. I certainly didn't mean to get you . . .

SENIOR SUBALTERN. (*Paces to* MILLINGTON.) Will you be quiet, sir?! I don't know what the hell your game is, Millington, but let me tell you this! If you put up one more black mark against me, I'll make damned sure you're kicked out of this Regiment. Now you hear me?!

MILLINGTON. Yes, Fothergill.

SENIOR SUBALTERN. Mr. Fothergill.

MILLINGTON. Mr. Fothergill.

SENIOR SUBALTERN. (*Backs two steps.*) Very well. Let's get you over to your quarters. Move!

(*They go off,* L. *arch, the* SENIOR SUBALTERN *last. The SOUND of CHARGING HORSES. The LIGHTS CHANGE to EVENING SETTING.* PRADAH SINGH, *magnificent in mess dress, comes on—directs the* MESS WAITERS, *also in mess kit, in straightening the furniture.* OFFSTAGE: *Relatively DISTANT HUNTING CRIES and SHOUTING . . .*)

ACT ONE

Scene 2

The Mess. The MESS NIGHT. PRADAH SINGH *claps hands, the* WAITERS *run off* R. *One* WAITER *stays in view at the side. The* SECOND IN COMMAND *and* SENIOR SUBALTERN *come on, both in "Duty" dress with swords.*

ROACH. (*Enters* D. L. *arch, crosses* R.) Well, Richard. Brandy?

SENIOR SUBALTERN. (*Follows in.*) Please, sir.

ROACH. Two brandies, please, Pradah Singh. (*Sits* R. C. *chair.*)

PRADAH. Sahib. (*Signals to* WAITER, *who will bring them to him on a tray.*)

ROACH. Well, sit down, my boy, sit down.

SENIOR SUBALTERN. Thank you, sir. (*They sit.* OFFSTAGE: *LAUGHTER, HUNTING CRIES come closer.* SENIOR SUBALTERN *smiles, sits* D. R. *chair.*) Sounds as if the game's in full cry, sir.

ROACH. Yes. (*Smiles.*) One of the penalties of being Officer of the Day on a Mess Night, um?

SENIOR SUBALTERN. Well, it's better than being Officer of the Week, sir. At least I shall be free for the ball on Saturday.

ROACH. Well, I shan't pretend that I mind too greatly about that. (PRADAH SINGH *brings drinks.*)

PRADAH. (*Crosses to* R. *of him.*) Your brandy, sahib.

ROACH. Thank you, Pradah Singh.

PRADAH. (*Crosses to* L. *of* FOTHERGILL.) Sahib.

SENIOR SUBALTERN. Thank you.

ROACH. Your health, Richard.

SENIOR SUBALTERN. And yours, sir. Thank you. (*They drink.*)

(OFFSTAGE: *A sudden loud BURST OF SHOUTING*

ACT I CONDUCT UNBECOMING 21

and LAUGHTER, very close. Then LT. HUTTON *runs in from* R., *dragging behind him what is in fact a stuffed boar on wheels or rollers, attached to a sort of metal broom handle by which he pulls it. He runs across and off* L. *arch, shouting . . .*)

HUTTON. Oink, oink—chaaaaarrge!

(*Almost at once the pursuing body comes through after him*—WIMBORNE *and* ADJUTANT *in lead, closely followed by* COLONEL, LTS. WINTERS *and* HART, BOULTON—*and the* DOCTOR, *trailing, out of condition. All are in mess dress:* WIMBORNE *and* ADJUTANT [*like* HART]. *They carry drawn swords* [*Senior Officers*] *or lances. They charge across, off* L.)

WIMBORNE. (*Followed by* BOULTON, *who stops in* L. *arch, runs* L. *after* HUTTON. FOTHERGILL *crosses* U. R. *of* ROACH.) There he goes . . . !
BOULTON. (*Crosses* L. *stops* L. C.) Charge!
HART. (*From* R. *to* C. *veranda.*) Charge! Come on, sir—down by the card room.
WINTERS. (*Enters* R. *doors, shouts at foot of steps.*) Where is he?
BOULTON. Flagstaff, man! Come on! (*Exits* D. L. *followed by* WIMBORNE.)
WINTERS. Charge!
ADJUTANT. After the devil! Charge!
HART. Get him! Charge!
COLONEL. Up the Regiment . . . ! (*Enters doors* R., *exits* D. L.)
DOCTOR. (*Enters doors* R., *exits* D. L. *Puffing.*) My word, Colonel, we'll have to find someone slower next time . . . ! (*He is last off.* SENIOR SUBALTERN *laughs.*)
SENIOR SUBALTERN. I rather think the Doctor's past his best for the game, sir!
ROACH. Well, I suppose it is his job to keep us fit, rather than himself, um?

(*Now* Lt. Truly *hobbles on from the doors* r., *far behind, one leg strapped-up, clutching a lance, wobbling about, panting.*)

Truly. (*Stops* c.) Which way did they go?!
Senior Subaltern. Down towards the flagstaff, old man!
Truly. (*Crosses* l.) Ah! Charge . . . ! (*Hobbles* l., *waving lance, collapses table,* d. l.)
Roach. For heaven's sake, Truly—don't damage that leg of yours any further.
Truly. Never fear, sir!—Charge! (*Hobbles off* l.)
Senior Subaltern. Johnny's a goer, sir.
Roach. Yes. Richard, I wanted to ask you about your two new charges. Has there been any improvement there?
Senior Subaltern. (*Breaks* d. r.) Not much, sir. He let the Colonel's new string of ponies escape yesterday.
Roach. Millington?
Senior Subaltern. (*Turns.*) Yes, sir. We got them together again. By nightfall.
Roach. (*Shakes head.*) It won't do. Won't do.
Senior Subaltern. (*Sits* d. r. *chair.*) Couldn't we—get rid of him, sir?
Roach. Of course we could. Wouldn't look good, though, would it? General's son. Colonel of the Regiment. . . . (OFFSTAGE: *SOUNDS of "HUNT" circling Mess.* Roach *rises.* Fothergill *rises.*) Extraordinary business. (*Looks at portrait.* OFFSTAGE: *Sudden burst of animated cheering and shouting, much closer.* Roach *crosses* d. r. *of* r. c. *table.*) Richard, did you notice Millington was drinking too much at dinner tonight?
Senior Subaltern. Yes, sir. But strictly speaking, there's no ruling about that, as long as he can hold it.
Roach. (*Crosses to him.*) All the same, I think you should remove him as quickly and quietly as you can from the Mess tonight.
Senior Subaltern. (*Rises.*) Right, sir.

(Hutton *comes charging through again,* r. *doors, drag-*

ging the boar, ADJUTANT, WIMBORNE *and* WINTERS *close at his heels.*)

WIMBORNE. (*Stabs and misses.*) Nearly got him . . . !
HUTTON. Hell . . . ! (HUTTON *SKIDS and falls* D. L. *The others at once close round the boar, sinking swords and lances into its hind quarters.*)
WIMBORNE. Aha—yes! (*Sinks in sword.*) A point!
ADJUTANT. (*Stabs.*) A point!
WIMBORNE. (*Stabs again, breaks* D. R. C. FOTHERGILL *and* ROACH *break* U.—FOTHERGILL *to showcase,* ROACH *to* U. L. C. *pillar.*) A veritable point!
WINTERS. (*Stabs.*) Hooray!

(*The joke is evidently to stab the boar only in the hind quarters, this being the area presented in "flight."* DRAKE *followed by* MILLINGTON *has now appeared on the veranda from off* U. R., *watching.* HART *scrambles up as the others stab and stab again.*)

HUTTON. Hey—hang off, you chaps!
WIMBORNE. A point!
ADJUTANT. And another!   (*Together.*)
HUTTON. You're cheating!
WINTERS. Another!
WIMBORNE. What do you mean, cheating, sir?! (*Breaks* R.)

(BOULTON, DOCTOR *and* COLONEL *enter, puffing badly.*)

HUTTON. (*Rises.*) I slipped! I fell!
ADJUTANT. (*Breaks* D. L.) Stay on your ruddy feet, then!
HUTTON. The hell with you, then! Charge! (HUTTON *seizes handle, starts off* L. *Three* SUBALTERNS *start off* L. *again.*)
WIMBORNE. (*Starts* L.) Aha—he's away . . . !
ADJUTANT. (*Starts* L.) Chaaarrge . . . ! (*They start in pursuit.*)

COLONEL. (*Enters* R. *doors to* C. *with* DOCTOR.) No, no, gentlemen, I pray you . . . ! Your Colonel is old—too old . . . !
WIMBORNE. Never, Colonel!
ADJUTANT. Perish the thought, Colonel!   (*Together.*)
WINTERS. Shame, Colonel!
BOULTON. Shame . . .
COLONEL. (*Panting, chuckles. Crosses* R., *sits his chair.*) I thank you for your kind thoughts, gentlemen. But really, the Doctor and I are quite exhausted for this evening. (*Sheaths sword, sits, hands sword to* PRADAH. PRADAH *takes* WIMBORNE'S *and* DOCTOR'S *swords.*) Eh, Doctor?

(ROACH *crosses* R. *of* R. C. *chair.*)

DOCTOR. (*From top step crosses to* C. *chair.*) I must—second the motion, Colonel. (*Sinks into chair.*) I prescribe—drinks for the Mess. (*CHEER.*)
COLONEL. An excellent suggestion. Pradah Singh.
PRADAH. Very good, Colonel.

(PRADAH SINGH *motions to* WAITERS, *who serve the company.* PRADAH SINGH *will serve only* COLONEL *and* WIMBORNE, *and assist* COLONEL *and* SENIOR OFFICERS *with cigars.* HART "*parks*" *boar upstage, others "park" their lances.*)

COLONEL. Well, Lionel . . . Alastair . . . what was the final score?
HUTTON. (*Enters* L., *crosses to* C. *Quickly.*) It was a draw, Colonel!
HART. A draw!?
WINTERS. Rubbish!
BOULTON. What?!
HUTTON. Oh, rubbish!
WIMBORNE. A draw?! What the blazes do you mean, a draw, sir?!

ADJUTANT. It was a walkover, Colonel—six valid points at least! (*Agreement.*)

WIMBORNE. (*Crosses* R. *to* D. R. *chair.*) At least six—more like a dozen!

HART. But I slipped—fell down!

WIMBORNE. (*Sits.* PRADAH *gives him drink.*) You shouldn't drink so much, then! (BOULTON *crosses* L. *of* HUTTON. *Laughter. All very good-natured, this argument.*)

HUTTON. Colonel, sir—I appeal to you. Surely it doesn't count if the runner falls down, Colonel? (*Breaks* U., *gets drink from* HART.)

WIMBORNE. Of course it does!

ADJUTANT. Whyever shouldn't it?

HUTTON. (*Moves in* D. C.) A ruling, Colonel.

COLONEL. I'm not gifted with the wisdom of Solomon, gentlemen. (*Cries of "shame!":* WINTERS, BOULTON, HART.) Lionel, a ruling is required on the Mess sport.

ROACH. (*Crosses* D. R. *of* R. C. *table.*) Well, Colonel, I suggest . . . "should the runner be incapacitated, there shall be allowed, during the period of his incapacitation, one valid point only." (*Sits* R. C. *chair.*)

HUTTON. Here, here!

WIMBORNE. Disgusting . . . !

ADJUTANT and OTHERS. Shame . . . ! Shame . . . ! Shame . . . !

HUTTON. Carried unanimously, Colonel! (*Crosses to* D. L. *of* R. C. *table.*)

COLONEL. (HART *crosses* U. L. *to other* SUBALTERNS. *Amused:*) Very well, Mister Hutton. I declare a draw.

HUTTON. Thank you, Colonel.

WINTERS. "Oy-oy-oink."

WIMBORNE. Well, anyway, it was a damned fine run.

(TRULY *limps on from* D. L. *to* C. *during "Here, here."*)

TRULY. Did you catch him alright?!

WINTERS. Look who's here! Late again. (EVERYBODY *laughs.*)

(MILLINGTON *and* DRAKE *move* L. *to* L. *arch.* MILLINGTON *comes in,* DRAKE *tries to pull him out, to no avail.*)

WIMBORNE. (*Grinning.*) Where the devil have you been?!

ADJUTANT. Making an inspection of the lines, have you, John? (*Gets cigar lit.*)

TRULY. I've got a handicap, dammit. (*Indicates leg.*)

COLONEL. Come on, young Truly, sit down——you'll ruin that leg of yours.

TRULY. (*To attention.* WIMBORNE *puts glass on cabinet, crosses* L. *to him.*) It's perfectly alright, Colonel, I do assure you.

WIMBORNE. Don't argue with the Colonel, you young puppy. Come on! (WIMBORNE, *massively strong, lifts* TRULY *as though he were no weight at all and dumps him, gently in fact, into a chair* D. R. *to a cheer and laughter. There is much warmth and affection in all this boisterousness. This is their world.* WIMBORNE *crosses to chair between* ROACH *and* COLONEL—*sits, with glass.* DRAKE *and* MILLINGTON, D. L. *now, are very much out of it, though* DRAKE *tries to appear in.*)

TRULY. (*Gasps.*) Thank you, sir! (WINTERS *crosses to* L. C. *table, lights cigar.*)

MILLINGTON. (*Clutches* DRAKE'S *arm, sotto.*) What an —absolutely extraordinary performance, my dear fellow.

DRAKE. (*Brushes hand away.*) Be quiet.

MILLINGTON. (*Murmurs, grabs him.*) Don't take your arm away. . . . (*Is very, very drunk, but not obviously so.*)

COLONEL. Well now, Adjutant, I think it's about time the junior officers entertained the old codgers . . .

ROACH. (*To* FOTHERGILL:) Get Millington out, will you?

(FOTHERGILL *crosses* L., *puts glass* L. C. *table.*)

WIMBORNE. (*Sinks into chair.*) Here, here . . .

Doctor. Splendid idea, Colonel . . .
Adjutant. (*Crosses to* L. *of* Doctor—*turns to* Boulton.) I'm sure Mister Boulton would be happy to oblige with a dramatic recitation, Colonel.

(Hart *and* Winters *push* Boulton D. R. C. Wimborne *and* Doctor *rise,* Roach, *slight rise.* Hutton *pulls* Wimborne's *and* Roach's *chairs back six inches.*)

Wimborne. (*Claps.*) Approbation for Mister Boulton, gentlemen . . .

(Adjutant *pulls* Doctor's *chair back nine inches. They all clap, laughing.* Second in Command *motions to* Senior Subaltern *who works around towards* Millington. Hart *and* Winters *back to* L. C. *table.*)

Boulton. Oh, I say, look here, it was me last time.
Hutton. And it's you this time, Mr. Boulton!
Boulton. What about Johnno? (*Crosses to him.* Fothergill *crosses* D. L. *to* Millington.)
Truly. (*Clapping.*) Gammy leg, old man.
Wimborne. (*Laughing.*) Carry on, Mister Boulton. . . .
Boulton. (*Desperate, turns, crosses* L. C.) Well—what about the new chaps?

(Senior Subaltern, *having reached* Millington, *looks to* Second in Command. *Slight pause.*)

Wimborne. That's an idea.
Boulton. And a damned good one too. (*Crosses* U. L., *threatens* Hart *and* Winters.)
Wimborne. (*Rises.*) Colonel. Have I your permission to call upon the new men? (Drake *can't get* Millington *to go. Slight pause.*)
Roach. (*Murmurs.*) Perhaps a little soon, Colonel . . .
Colonel. Oh, I don't see why, Lionel. It is Plassey Week, after all. Yes, carry on, Alastair . . . why not?

WIMBORNE. Thank you, Colonel. (*Crosses* D. L. *of* C.) You, sir—forward march. (DRAKE *nudges* MILLINGTON *who doesn't hear.* WIMBORNE *points to* C.) Here. (*Indicates to step forward.*)

(*It is of course* MILLINGTON, *though he doesn't take it in.* SENIOR SUBALTERN *hisses at him.*)

SENIOR SUBALTERN. Go on, man—move! (*Gives* MILLINGTON *a discreet shove.* MILLINGTON *lurches silghtly, advances with the stiff formality of the very drunk.*)

WIMBORNE. Come on, sir—double time! (*Crosses* R. *to his chair.*)

MILLINGTON. (*Crosses to* C.) Sir. (*Stands facing* WIMBORNE.)

WIMBORNE. (*Sits.*) Address yourself to the Colonel, sir.

MILLINGTON. Yes, sir. (*Faces* COLONEL. *His eyes have the very open, earnest stare. His reactions are just a little delayed. The others have drunk enough to miss this.*) Colonel, sir.

COLONEL. What is your name, sir?

MILLINGTON. . . . Millington, sir.

COLONEL. Millington. Yes. General Millington's boy.

MILLINGTON. . . . Yes, sir. Colonel.

COLONEL. We want you to entertain us, Mister Millington. What are you going to do? (*Silence.*) Um? Well? Speak up, speak up.

MILLINGTON. (*Solemnly.*) . . . Sing a song, Colonel. (*Laughter, ad libs.* FOTHERGILL *gets chair from* U. L., *sits in it in front of* D. L. *table.* DRAKE D. *of him, standing.* BOULTON *on carver from* U. L., *to arch* L., *sits.* HART *moves chair forward for* ADJUTANT *from* R. *of* U. L. *table, stands behind him.* WINTERS *sits on* L. C. *table.*)

COLONEL. A song. Alright. Good. Carry on, Mister Millington.

WIMBORNE. It'll make a change from all those damned recitations. (*Laughter.* WIMBORNE *sits.* MILLINGTON *straightens, takes a deep breath, shuts his eyes and sings.*)

MILLINGTON. "Plaisir d'amour . . ."
WIMBORNE. It's a bloody Froggy song. (*Laughter.*)
MILLINGTON. ". . . ne dure qu'un moment . . ."
ADJUTANT. (HART *laughs.*) Sing up, Mister Millington!
HART. Come on, man. Don't be shy, Millington.
BOULTON. Yes, come on—we can't hear you.
WINTERS. You're whispering.
MILLINGTON. "Chagrin d'amour dure toute . . ."
HUTTON. Louder!
BOULTON. (*Stamping.*) Sing louder, man . . . !
(*Laughter.*)
HART. Boooo!

(HUTTON *laughs.*)

MILLINGTON. ". . . la vi—e."
WINTERS. (*Rises—loud:*) Let's hear you, Mister Millington!
ROACH. (*Rises, gestures—then sits.*) Shh . . .

(*Throughout this traditional barracking,* MILLINGTON *has sung on, oblivious, as he now does, in a sweet, clear, perfect voice.*)

MILLINGTON.
"J'ai tout quitte pour l'ingrate Sylvie;
Elle me quitte et prend un autre amant"
(*They listen in absolute stillness and silence now to the sweet voice in the night.*)
"Plaisir d'amour
ne dure qu'un moment:
Chagrin d'amour dure toute
la vi—e."

(MILLINGTON *draws the final notes right away into nothing. Silence. Stillness. A shifting, almost of embarrassment. Then the* COLONEL *taps in gentle ap-*

plause on his leg. Others applaud. WIMBORNE *applauds properly with hands, as do* SUBALTERNS.)

COLONEL. Well done, Mister Millington.
DOCTOR. Well sung.
WIMBORNE. Well sung indeed, young man.
ROACH. Very good, Mister Millington. (*Visible relief from* SECOND IN COMMAND, DRAKE, SENIOR SUBALTERN.)
MILLINGTON. Colonel, sir.
COLONEL. Yes, Mister Millington?
MILLINGTON. Permission to pass out, Colonel. (*Drops like a stone at the* COLONEL'S *feet, dead drunk. Shocked, stunned silence.*)
COLONEL. (*Rises, turns away.*) Well, really! (*All others rise.*)
ROACH. (*Rising.*) Mister Harper!
ADJUTANT. Mister Fothergill!
SENIOR SUBALTERN. (*One pace forward.*) Sir!
ADJUTANT. Remove this officer to his quarters, sir!
SENIOR SUBALTERN. (FOTHERGILL *clicks at* DRAKE *to help. They kneel*—FOTHERGILL U., DRAKE D., *pull him up.*) Sir!
ADJUTANT. (*As they lift* MILLINGTON.) I shall speak to you in the morning, Mister Fothergill.
SENIOR SUBALTERN. (BOULTON *moves armchair* U.) . . . Sir. (*They drag him off* L.)

(WINTERS *crosses* D. L. HART *crosses* L. BOULTON *turns.* ADJUTANT *crosses* U. *onto* R. *steps. Only now does* COLONEL *turn back, angry and contemptuous.*)

COLONEL. (*Starts* L. *and* U. C. WIMBORNE *crosses* D. R. *to* TRULY.) Perhaps you'd join me on the veranda, Lionel?
ROACH. (*Follows* L. *of* COLONEL.) Thank you, Colonel. I'd like that.
DOCTOR. (*Crosses* D. *to* WIMBORNE. *Disgusted.*) Gentlemen who cannot hold their liquor shouldn't drink.
WIMBORNE. (*Turns. Rather amused.*) He did finish his song, Doctor. You must allow him that.

COLONEL. (*Stops* U. C.) I do not find it amusing, Alastair. (*All to attention.*)
WIMBORNE. I'm sorry, Colonel. (COLONEL *starts up* C. *steps.*)
HUTTON. (*Bravely steps in.*) Colonel, sir.
COLONEL. (*Turns to him.*) Yes, Mister Hutton?
HUTTON. May I have the honour to challenge you to a match at billiards, Colonel?

(*Silence. They wait the* COLONEL'S *reaction. He looks at all.*)

COLONEL. Very well, young man. (*Turns to go off* R. *Then, relaxing all round:*) If you want another caning . . . (*Crosses* R. *to steps—*DOCTOR *crosses to showcase.*)
WIMBORNE. (*Crosses* L. *to* L. C. *table.*) I'll lay a pony on the Colonel. Any takers? (SUBALTERNS *ad lib.*)
HART. What about me!
COLONEL. (*All stop ad libs.*) Now, Alastair. You know we don't allow gaming in the Mess. (*Turns at steps.*)
WIMBORNE. No, Colonel.
COLONEL. Not in front of the Colonel, anyway.
WIMBORNE. (*Grins, relaxes.*) No, Colonel. (HART *crosses to* ROACH. *Starts exit veranda* L. *All laugh.*)
TRULY. (*Crosses* D. L. *of* R. C. *table.*) Colonel, sir.
COLONEL. Yes, Mister Truly?
TRULY. Permission to fall out, Colonel.
COLONEL. Leg troubling you?
TRULY. Just a bit, Colonel.
COLONEL. (HART *crosses* U. *to veranda.* BOULTON *takes his place.*) Right. Get to bed then.
TRULY. Thank you, Colonel. (*Crosses* L. *to arch.*)
COLONEL. Doctor, I'd much appreciate it if you'd take a look at— (TRULY *gives a cry and falls, table* D. L.)
DOCTOR. Of course, Colonel. (*Crosses to* TRULY.)
TRULY. Sorry, Colonel! (*In evident pain. Slightest pause.* WIMBORNE *strides across.*)
WIMBORNE. (*Turns.*) Come on, young man! (*He gathers him up into his arms.*)

TRULY. (DOCTOR *breaks to* C.) It isn't necessary, sir, I assure you.

WIMBORNE. Be quiet, sir. Where do you want him, Doctor?

DOCTOR. (*Puts glass on* R. C. *table.*) His own quarters, I think.

WIMBORNE. Right! With your permission, Colonel.

COLONEL. Thank you, Alastair. (*Turns to go*—HUTTON *and* ADJUTANT *open doors.* WIMBORNE *strides out* L., *carrying* TRULY. DOCTOR *starts* L.) Well, Mister Hutton. Let's see if you've learned anything since our last encounter.

HUTTON. Right, Colonel. (*About to go off* R., *the* COLONEL *turns back, halting the* DOCTOR *at* L., *across stage.*)

COLONEL. (*Turns back.*) Oh, Doctor.

DOCTOR. (*Stops in arch.*) Yes, Colonel?

COLONEL. Perhaps you'd better take a look at the other young gentleman.

DOCTOR. I will indeed, Colonel. (*Exits* L.)

(*They go off,* COLONEL R. *LIGHTS FADE and CHANGE TO BRIGHT MORNING SETTING.*)

ACT ONE

SCENE 3

The Mess. The next morning. MILLINGTON *limps on,* D. L., *heavily hungover. Pale-faced and taut, crosses to* L. C. *table—stumbles, crosses to* D. L. *table, buttoning, checks empty bottle, turns* U. *to* L. C. *table. He limps to chair, sinks into it. Gathers his strength to call.*

MILLINGTON. (*A whisper.*) Pradah Singh . . . (*He tries again: a croak.*) Pradah Singh . . . !

(PRADAH SINGH *enters* R. *doors.*)

PRADAH. (*Crosses to* L. *of* C.—L. C. *table.*) Good morning, sahib.

MILLINGTON. Whiskey, Pradah Singh.

PRADAH. If I may say.

MILLINGTON. Large, large . . .

PRADAH. It is, perhaps, a trifle early, sahib.

MILLINGTON. Don't make me argue, there's a good fellow.

PRADAH. No, sahib. (MILLINGTON *is too still. Concerned,* PRADAH SINGH *fetches drink from behind* L. C. *pillar. Crosses back to* R. *of* MILLINGTON.) Your whiskey, sahib.

MILLINGTON. (*Hands trembling,* MILLINGTON *takes drink, gags on it, gets it down. His body shudders as the "shakes" depart. A silence.*) I needed that.

PRADAH. (*Sadly.*) . . . Yes, sahib.

MILLINGTON. (*Puts glass on tray. Sharply.*) Thank you, Pradah Singh. (*Sits* U. L. C. *corner.*)

(PRADAH SINGH *exits* D. L. *as* DRAKE *comes on, at the end of his tether, coldly enraged.* MILLINGTON *re-adopts his flippant manner.*)

DRAKE. (*Enters veranda* L.) Where the devil have you been, Millington? I've been searching everywhere for you. (*Crosses to* R. *of him.*)

MILLINGTON. My dear fellow, good morning.

DRAKE. You realise we're due here at eight for the Senior Subaltern.

MILLINGTON. I am here, Arthur.

DRAKE. (*Turns to him.*) Don't be flippant with me!

MILLINGTON. (*Crosses* D. L. *Winces.*) . . . I wish you wouldn't shout, old chap. (*Rises and moves* D. L., *retreating.*)

(*Silence.*)

DRAKE. (*Follows him.*) Why did you ever come here, Millington?

MILLINGTON. (*Smiles, sits* D. L. *chair.*) Oh, one cannot escape one's destiny, my dear fellow. One must go through the motions of failure—

DRAKE. (D. L. C. *Crosses to him.*) Then, let me warn you, Millington. I have never in my life wanted anything but to be a part of this Regiment. I do not intend to have that ambition destroyed by you. If necessary, I shall resort to physical means to protect it. Do you understand me?

MILLINGTON. (*Astonished.*) My dear fellow, you are never referring to fisticuffs, surely.

DRAKE. (*Breaks to* D. R. C. *table—gets hat.*) What do you think I am referring to, Mister Millington?

(*The* SENIOR SUBALTERN *storms on,* R. *doors. Where* DRAKE *has been bitingly cold, he is ablaze with rage.* MILLINGTON *appears dazed.*)

SENIOR SUBALTERN. (*Crosses* L. *of* C.) Millington! Come here! Come here!

MILLINGTON. (*Rises.*) . . . Yes, Mister Fothergill.

SENIOR SUBALTERN. Move, man! Move! (MILLINGTON *speeds up. The* SENIOR SUBALTERN *trembles with anger. When* MILLINGTON *stands before him, he stamps attention. He raises his cane just short of* MILLINGTON'S *face. One feels he might at any moment strike.*) I have just been up before the Adjutant because of you! Now once more, Millington—once more—so help me, I will give you such a thrashing— Within an inch of your life! You hear me?!

MILLINGTON. (*Subdued.*) Yes, Mister Fothergill.

SENIOR SUBALTERN. (*Seizes* MILLINGTON'S *jacket,* L. *hand, swings him round, and* U.—*slams him against* R. C. *pillar. Facing* D., *drags* MILLINGTON.) Come here, Millington! I want to show you something! (*Pitches* MILLINGTON *almost off his feet, up onto the veranda.* FOTHERGILL *on top step of veranda. He throws him against an upright and, from behind, yanks* MILLINGTON'S *head round by the hair so that he looks off* L.) Now you see it?! Do you, Millington?! You see that—that structure?! That frame?!

MILLINGTON. Yes, Mister Fothergill.

SENIOR SUBALTERN. (*Releases hair.*) That is a whipping-post, Mister Millington! That is where they flogged sepoys in '57! And that is where you're going to find yourself, Mister Millington! You understand me?! You hear?! Out there! In that frame! (*This disturbs* DRAKE. *It goes too far.* MILLINGTON *covers face with hands.* SENIOR SUBALTERN *cuffs him in passing, shoves him* D. L. *of* C.) You hear me?! Do you?!

(MILLINGTON *comes down off veranda onto his knees. Opens his hands. He has been covering not fear, but a terrible, sweet smile. He chuckles slightly.* FOTHERGILL *follows a bit.*)

MILLINGTON. Oh, my dear fellow . . . The whip holds no terrors for me. No terrors at all.

(*Chilling. Silence.* SENIOR SUBALTERN, *quieter, colder, comes down,* U. L. *of* MILLINGTON. SENIOR SUBALTERN *starts to strike him with crop, controls himself.* DRAKE *is uncomfortable.*)

SENIOR SUBALTERN. We'll see, Mister Millington. We'll see.

DRAKE. (*Disturbed,* D. L.) . . . Mister Fothergill was speaking—figuratively, of course.

SENIOR SUBALTERN. Mister Fothergill was speaking literally, Mister Drake. The whip has been used on a difficult subaltern in recent times. No doubt it will be again.

DRAKE. . . . I see.

MILLINGTON. (*Rises* R., *a step.*) Who was the lucky man?

SENIOR SUBALTERN. That doesn't concern you. Now

listen to me, both of you. (*Both come to attention.*) The Adjutant has instructed me to inform you officially, that if he receives one more report of unsatisfactory behaviour by either one of you, that man's service will be terminated at once. (*Points crop.*) You, Mr. Millington, will cut down on your drinking. As to the ball tonight, the Colonel has reluctantly given permission for you both to wear Mess Dress. You will both prove yourselves worthy of that honour. You will both now put on your best jodhpurs and tunics and report to Sgt. Major Lang. The stables need mucking out. MOVE—!

DRAKE. (*Breaks a step* U.) Mister . . .
SENIOR SUBALTERN. (*Turns to* DRAKE.) Move!

(DRAKE *goes* L. *followed by* MILLINGTON.)

MILLINGTON. (*Already moving.*) Yes, Mister Fothergill . . .

(SENIOR SUBALTERN *watches a moment, leaves via veranda,* R. *LIGHTS FADE TO EVENING SETTING* [*perhaps* SERVANTS, *at* PRADAH'S *direction, move chairs back to "open up" the set*].)

ACT ONE

SCENE 4

The Mess. The night of the ball. MUSIC from up off L. *The ball is in progress on the Plain, situated mainly* U. L. *offstage. The impression is of catching glimpses as characters return from time to time to the Mess buildings.* WAITERS *move about with trays of champagne.* OTHER GUESTS *are occasionally seen passing.*

Check WAITER'S *cue sheets: as candle reaches* D. L.: *three* CROWS *on from* R. *doors on top step.* HUTTON *enters D. L. arch, stands D. L. as* CROWS *cross to him. He bows and kisses hand of each in turn. On second hand kiss* PRADAH *claps.* WAITERS *take stole, give to* PRADAH *who gives to* WAITER *on steps*—PRADAH *then stands U. end top step.* HUTTON *points L. They exit. As first* CROW *turns L.—cue light for* WIMBORNE *party.*

All officers, including MILLINGTON *and* DRAKE, *wear full Mess Dress—except the* SECOND IN COMMAND, *Officer of the Week, and* HART, *Officer of the Day.* HART *and* SENIOR OFFICERS *wear swords.* SUBALTERNS *do not. The* WOMEN *are beautifully gowned. Open on empty stage. A shout of laughter, and a group*—WIMBORNE, TRULY, BOULTON *and* WINTERS, *of which* MRS. HASSELTINE *is the centre of attention —comes onto veranda.*

WIMBORNE. (*Leads* MRS. HASSELTINE *to pillar* U. R. C.) My dear Marge, you really are an outrageous woman!

WINTERS. It's a damned funny story, though, sir, you must admit!

WIMBORNE. (*Amused, turns, pushes* WINTERS *off* L.) And you, sir, are far too young! Get away! Get away!

MRS. HASSELTINE. (*Crosses* D. C., *followed by men.*) Now you really must allow me a moment or two to rest, gentlemen.

BOULTON. Shame . . .   TRULY. Shame . . .

WINTERS. (*Enters arch* L. *Picks up champagne. Kneels* L. *of* MRS. HASSELTINE, *offers glass.* CROWS *enter onto veranda from* L.) May I have the pleasure of the first dance on your return, ma'am? (*Puts crop on* L. C. *table.*)

WIMBORNE. (*Gets drink.*) Insubordination, sir!

MRS. HASSELTINE. You're too young. Your Squadron Commander says so.

WIMBORNE. Quite right, Marge. (WINTERS *rises.*)

BOULTON. (*Kisses her hand.*) Is one ever too young to appreciate wit and beauty, Mrs. Hasseltine?

Mrs. Hasseltine. For that, I might consider it.

Wimborne. (*Draws sword, bangs floor, starts* D. R. *after* Boulton. Truly *and* Winters *run round* L. C. *table,* Hart *and* Boulton *round* R. C. *table.* Mrs. Hasseltine *crosses* R. *to medal case, puts glass down.* Crows *hide in mock fright round* U. R. C. *pillar.*) You lecherous young devil. (*Draws sword.*) Away with you—the pack of you! (*Jokingly waves sword about his head.* Subalterns *retreat laughing.* Colonel *comes onto veranda from off* L.—*to* C. *veranda.*)

Colonel. In heaven's name, Alastair. You're not decapitating our subalterns, are you?

Wimborne. (*Has got to below* U. R. C. *pillar. Sheaths sword.*) Defending a lady's honour, Colonel.

Mrs. Hasseltine. (*Crosses to* R. C. *chair, sits.*) A pardonable exaggeration, Colonel.

Colonel. (*Crosses* D. *to her.*) You're a wicked woman, Marge, but you look splendid. (Wimborne *crosses* D. R. *of* Mrs. Hasseltine, *sits arm of* Colonel's *chair.* Subalterns *are now* D. L. *and* L.)

Mrs. Hasseltine. (Truly *hands* Boulton *two glasses;* Truly, Hart, Winters *each take glasses.*) I hope to remain so, Colonel, but your young gentlemen won't release me. (Two Crows *exit* L. "*Redhair*" *stays* C.)

(Wimborne *and* Subalterns *laugh. The MUSIC STOPS, clapping offstage. The* Colonel, *amused, turns with mock severity on* Subalterns.)

Colonel. (*Turns to* Subalterns—Boulton *hands him glass.* Wimborne *talks to* Mrs. Hasseltine.) What are you young gentlemen doing here? The Second in Command and I have scoured the country for partners for you. All the most eligible and attractive young ladies in the district await you on the Plain. (Hart, Winters *and* Truly *bow and toast "Redhair" who smiles and exits* L.)

Boulton. You're never referring to the "Crows,"

Colonel? (MRS. HASSELTINE *and* WIMBORNE *laugh delightedly.*)

COLONEL. To your duties, gentlemen. Quick march.

BOULTON. (*Shoves glass in* WINTERS *hand.*) Oh, Lord. Bags I the one with the red hair! (*Suddenly dashes off veranda,* L.)

WINTERS. (*Shoves glass in* TRULY'S *hand. Exits veranda* L.—HART *follows.* TRULY *puts three glasses on* WAITER'S *tray and exits* L. *arch.* WIMBORNE *playfully kicks* WINTERS *as he exits, and then crosses* D. L.) Hey—wait a bit! She's mine! (*Dashes after* BOULTON, TRULY *hobbling in rear. MUSIC STARTS again, rather quieter.*)

WIMBORNE. (*Crosses* D. L., *gets wing—*WAITER.) I know just how they feel, Colonel.

COLONEL. (C.) We met a goodly number of what may fairly be termed "Crows" ourselves, did we not?

WIMBORNE. (*Crosses to* L. C.) We did indeed, Colonel. It's Marge. She's spoiled them for anyone else.

MEM. (*Enters, veranda* C.) Colonel . . .

WIMBORNE. (*Bows.*) Evening, Mem.

(*As* MEM STRANG *comes to* COLONEL *on veranda.*)

MEM. (*Crosses* D. C.) Good evening. Colonel, dear, the guests . . .

COLONEL. Yes, yes, duty calls. (*Puts glass on table. Turns to* WIMBORNE. WIMBORNE *puts glass on* D. L. *table.*) I think we owe the ladies a turn or two, Alastair—if you will excuse us, my dear. (*Turns to* MRS. HASSELTINE.)

MRS. HASSELTINE. Of course, Colonel. (COLONEL *gives* MEM *his arm. They exit veranda,* L.)

WIMBORNE. (*Crosses to* C.) Sorry, Marge.

MRS. HASSELTINE. (*Meets him* C.) Don't be silly. They all want to dance with our dashing V.C.

WIMBORNE. Why don't you come with us?

MRS. HASSELTINE. (*They cross* U. *on to veranda.*) No, no, I think I'll sit out here and watch you doing your duty with the "Crows."

WIMBORNE. Oh Lord. Now there is an act deserves a medal if you like.

MRS. HASSELTINE. Get away with you. . . .

WIMBORNE. Shan't be long. . . . (*Follows* COLONEL *and* MEM *off veranda* L. MRS. HASSELTINE *crosses* L. *on veranda. Simultaneously a* WAITER *enters stage from* D. L. *with fresh tray of drinks, and* MILLINGTON *comes on from stage* R. *He does not see* MRS. HASSELTINE, *but she watches him.*)

MILLINGTON. (*Stops* WAITER D. C.) I say, just a moment, my dear fellow.

WAITER. Sahib . . .

(MILLINGTON *takes a drink. The* WAITER *attempts to move on.* MILLINGTON *grips edge of tray.*)

MILLINGTON. Ah— Ah— Ah— (*He downs first drink, returns glass. Takes second, downs that, replaces glass.* WAITER *starts* U. C. MILLINGTON *signals "stop."* MRS. HASSELTINE *moves* C. *on veranda as* MILLINGTON *downs second drink. As he takes third and fourth,* PRADAH *signals* D. L. WAITER *off* L. *and exits* R. *in disgust. Crosses* R. *to medal case. Puts one glass down, sips other. Bows.* WAITER *bows.*)

WAITER. Sahib . . . (MILLINGTON *goes* R. *to put aside fourth drink as* WAITER, *leaving via veranda, passes* MRS. HASSELTINE U. C. *on veranda.*) Mem sahib . . . ?

(*She says "thank you," takes glass.* WAITER *goes* L. MILLINGTON *turns. His charm is too calculated in this scene, too evidently scheming. Her attitude is ambiguous when not imperious.*)

MILLINGTON. (*Turns to her.*) Why . . . Mrs. Hasseltine.

MRS. HASSELTINE. Mister Millington, I believe.

MILLINGTON. (*Toasts her and bows.*) Your servant, ma'am.

MRS. HASSELTINE. (*Glancing outside.*) You should be

out dancing, Mister Millington. There are many young ladies on the plain would be glad of your company.

MILLINGTON. (*Crosses above* R. C. *chair.*) Tell me, ma'am. I know that they reverence the cow in India. Do they also reverence the crow?

MRS. HASSELTINE. (*Amused, crosses* D. *to* L. *of* C.) Some of them are very attractive.

MILLINGTON. It is pleasing, ma'am, to hear beauty pay tribute to mere attractiveness.

MRS. HASSELTINE. . . . Do you not think you have already paid me one compliment too many in public, Mister Millington?

MILLINGTON. (*Crosses a step to her.*) That is why I am taking such care to pay my future compliments in private, ma'am.

MRS. HASSELTINE. (*Crosses to* D. L. *table.*) You are to pay me no more compliments at all, Mister Millington. (*Smiles.*) At least, none that you could not as readily pay your mother. (*Puts glass down.*)

MILLINGTON. (*Crosses* D. L. *of* C.) Ah, well, she, poor lady, is dead.

MRS. HASSELTINE. (*Turns to him.*) I am sorry.

MILLINGTON. You have no reason to be, Mrs. Hasseltine. (*Looks at portrait, makes ironic toast.*) It is a compliment to her good sense. (*Makes slight toast to portrait. She follows his gaze. He finishes drink, takes up fourth.*)

MRS. HASSELTINE. (*Crosses* R. *to* C. *level with* MILLINGTON.) You know, you really shouldn't drink so much, Mister Millington.

MILLINGTON. (*Crosses* L. *to* C.) No, ma'am. No, I shouldn't.

MRS. HASSELTINE. (*Crosses to him.*) Particularly in the circumstances.

MILLINGTON. Ah. My reputation travels before me.

MRS. HASSELTINE. (*Turns head away.*) It is already quite extensive.

MILLINGTON. (*Smiles.*) . . . I should like to think we had something in common, Mrs. Hasseltine.

Mrs. Hasseltine. (*Looks at him. Severishly:*) It is a great mistake, Mister Millington, to be deceived by reputations.

Millington. Yes, Mrs. Hasseltine, it is. (*Turns R. Looks again at the portrait.*)

Mrs. Hasseltine. (*Crosses to L. of R. C. table.*) ... That is the second slighting remark you have made of your father.

Millington. (*Crosses R. to medals, puts glass down.*) Thoroughly well merited, I do assure you. He was a perfect swine.

Mrs. Hasseltine. That is not an attitude you will find appreciated here, Mister Millington. The General is revered in this Mess.

Millington. It was not a pronouncement to the Mess, Mrs. Hasseltine, but an aside to you.

Mrs. Hasseltine. (*Turns away.*) Under the impression, apparently, that it would fall on sympathetic ears.

Millington. (*Crosses to R. of R. C. table, one foot up.*) My sole impression of you, Mrs. Hasseltine, is that you are a woman.

Mrs. Hasseltine. (*Hard. Moves away, L. C.*) Don't be insolent, Mister Millington.

Millington. (*Crosses above table to U. R. of her.*) Forgive me. I had not thought the remark insolent. (*Sighs.*) Clearly you must have taken to my father.

Mrs. Hasseltine. I scarely knew him. He was a hard man. But never without cause. (*Turns D. L. of C.*)

Millington. (*Smiles. Crosses to L. C. table, picks up crop.*) I think you do him an injustice, Mrs. Hasseltine. I don't remember that he ever flogged me himself. We had an estates manager, Mister Radlett, who was adept at that particular function. A fine, free-flowing action. (*Crosses D. L. C., swings crop at her.*)

Mrs. Hasseltine. (*Jumps U. R. C., turns away.*) ... I doubt it was more than you deserved.

Millington. I wouldn't argue with that, ma'am. (*Crosses U. C. below step. Chuckles.*) What is amusing is that they are proposing to repeat the dose here. Did you know? Out there, (*Points off* U. L.) on that frame thing —strapping me up and walloping away.

MRS. HASSELTINE. (*Crosses* D. *to* R. *of* R. C. *table, puts fan on it.*) . . . I should derive what amusement you can from it now, Mister Millington. They will certainly do it if you compel them to.

MILLINGTON. I'm sure of that, ma'am.

MRS. HASSELTINE. (*Sits Colonel's chair.*) What they have done before, and recently, they will do again.

MILLINGTON. (*Crosses* R. *to above* R. C. *chair.*) What has escaped me, thus far, is the identify of the victim of that last occasion.

MRS. HASSELTINE. It was Mister Truly.

MILLINGTON. Ah. He of the gammy leg. (*She laughs.*) No wonder he is such an example to us all.

MRS. HASSELTINE. (*Evenly.*) Let us hope he will prove an example to you, Mister Millington. (*Leans over* L. *arm.*)

MILLINGTON. (*Moves* R. C. *chair* D. *and* R. *six inches—sits* R. *arm.*) Let us hope so. He must have done something spectacularly wicked to have been accorded such a privilege.

MRS. HASSELTINE. (*Evenly.*) He behaved stupidly towards me.

MILLINGTON. (*Quietly: inward.*) Yes. Yes, I wondered about that. (*Looks up. Smiles.*) Dear me. (*Rises, gets fan—proffers it to her.*) It appears that I shall have to restrain myself.

MRS. HASSELTINE. (*Rises, takes fan—he holds it. Drily.*) Yes, Mister Millington, you will.

MILLINGTON. It won't be easy, ma'am.

MRS. HASSELTINE. Steel yourself . . . (*Takes fan away from him.*) Good night, Mister Millington. (*She turns to go* L. *below table.*)

MILLINGTON. (*Sharply.*) No! (*Quickly smiles.*) No . . . Don't go. Please . . . (*She stops* U. C. *and turns, uncertain. MUSIC stops offstage. Clapping. Wandering about* D. R.) Did you know, it is said that when two pigeons mate, they mate for life? (*Picks up glass.*)

MRS. HASSELTINE. (*Crosses* D. C.) Really. (*Laugh.*)

MILLINGTON. Yes, so I have read.

MRS. HASSELTINE. (*Correct self.*) Oh, how touching, Mister Millington.

MILLINGTON. (*Crossing toward* R. C. *table.*) I must say, I find it rather sad.

MRS. HASSELTINE. Why?

MILLINGTON. Imagine if one were to die before the other.

MRS. HASSELTINE. (*Crosses in to table.*) That is why you drink. For a lost pigeon.

MILLINGTON. (*Smiles.*) Not really, ma'am—

MRS. HASSELTINE. Why, then?

MILLINGTON. (*Turns on her a sweet smile.*) Because I can't stop.

(*The MUSIC starts "Plaisir d'Amour" very softly from the darkness. A pause.*)

MRS. HASSELTINE. Is that—true?

MILLINGTON. Oh, don't concern yourself about it, please.

MRS. HASSELTINE. How old are you?

MILLINGTON. Twenty.

MRS. HASSELTINE. Then you have . . . (*Swings* L.)

MILLINGTON. "All life is before me," that's what they say.

MRS. HASSELTINE. (*Turns to him.*) Well, you certainly come to us laden with advantages, do you not?

MILLINGTON. But to you, it seems, I come with none. (*Moves towards her again above table.*) Am I quite out of favour?

MRS. HASSELTINE. (*Turning to go again* U. C.) Good night, Mister Millington. . . .

MILLINGTON. (*Holds her hand.*) Please. Mrs. Hasseltine—

ACT I   CONDUCT UNBECOMING   45

MRS. HASSELTINE. (*Breaks from him. Coldly:*) No. You will do yourself no good with this.

MILLINGTON. (*Follows* R. *of her. Slight smile.*) . . . As to that. We may differ.

(*Voices of* COLONEL, WIMBORNE *approach veranda.*)

WIMBORNE. (*Off.*) What do you think—is he right, Colonel? Will there be trouble on the frontier?

COLONEL. (*Off.*) Bound to be sooner or later, Alastair.

MRS. HASSELTINE. (*Points at him.*) . . . Stay away from me. (MRS. HASSELTINE *sweeps up to veranda as* COLONEL *and* WIMBORNE *come on.* MILLINGTON, *dejected, crosses* D. R., *sits Colonel's chair.*)

COLONEL. (*Entering* L. *of* WIMBORNE.) Ah, there you are, Marjorie.

MRS. HASSELTINE. (*Overbright.*) Duty done, Colonel?

COLONEL. For the moment, my dear, yes. You take Alastair away and dance with him. . . . It's my turn for a brief respite.

MRS. HASSELTINE. (R. *of* WIMBORNE.) With pleasure, Colonel . . .

WIMBORNE. Thank you, Colonel.

(MRS. HASSELTINE *and* WIMBORNE *leave veranda,* L. COLONEL *comes down* C. *steps. Sees* MILLINGTON. *Stops.*)

COLONEL. Good evening . . . Mister Millington.

MILLINGTON. (*Jumps to attention.*) . . . Good evening, Colonel.

COLONEL. (*Looks for rescue, but there is none.* MILLINGTON *now enjoys* COLONEL'S *discomfiture. A long silence.*) You, ah, enjoying yourself, Mister Millington?

MILLINGTON. Thank you, Colonel, yes.

COLONEL. Good, good. (*Silence. In desperation,* COLONEL *crosses to* L. C. *table, takes out cigar box. Then, feeling compelled to, offers case across stage to* MILLINGTON.) Do you, ah . . . ?

MILLINGTON. No, Colonel, thank you.

COLONEL. Very wise, very wise. (*Silence.* COLONEL *puts box down, prepares cigar.*)

MILLINGTON. Allow me to offer you a light, Colonel. (*Crosses to* R. *of him.*)

COLONEL. Oh, er, thank you. Thank you. (COLONEL *gets cigar going from* MILLINGTON'S *match.*) Thank you, Mister Millington. (*Silence.*)

MILLINGTON. They say a good subaltern always carries a box of matches and a spare handkerchief to a ball, Colonel.

COLONEL. Quite right. Quite right.

MILLINGTON. My father told me.

COLONEL. Yes. Yes. (*Silence.*) We, ah, we were all very sorry to hear of his death, you know. He was a fine man.

MILLINGTON. He was, Colonel. A great loss to the nation at large.

COLONEL. Just so. Just so. (*Looks at portrait.*) Sadly missed by all who knew him.

MILLINGTON. Sadly, Colonel. Sadly. (*Silence.*)

COLONEL. (*Turns to* MILLINGTON.) Well. You bear a fine name, Mister Millington.

MILLINGTON. I do, Colonel. I do.

COLONEL. (*Looks at him, frowns, turns away.*) Yes.

(*As* DRAKE *comes on, stops short, arch* L.)

DRAKE. Oh. (*Comes to attention.*) Good evening, Colonel.

COLONEL. Mister Drake. (*A silence.*) Well. Carry on, carry on. . . . (*Heads, relieved, for* R. *doors.*)

DRAKE. Thank you, Colonel.

MILLINGTON. . . . It's been a great pleasure speaking with you, Colonel.

COLONEL. (*Stops at bottom step, turns.*) . . . And you, Mister Millington. And you. (*Escapes* R. *doors from own Mess.*)

DRAKE. (*Crosses to him.*) What the devil have you been playing at?

MILLINGTON. (*Turns.*) My dear fellow. A little chat with the Colonel, nothing more.

DRAKE. Are you drunk?

MILLINGTON. Now is that kind, Arthur?

DRAKE. Are you?

MILLINGTON. I may have had one or two . . . (*Wanders to veranda* C.)

DRAKE. I think it's time we retired to our quarters.

MILLINGTON. (*Turns.*) I say. Do you think we should? Before the Colonel?

DRAKE. (*Crosses* R. *to steps.*) . . . I will get permission.

MILLINGTON. Very well, Arthur. Sleep well. I'm off dancing . . . ! (*Is gone, veranda* L., *before* DRAKE *can stop him.*)

DRAKE. Wait . . . Millington! Wait! (*Pursues* MILLINGTON.)

(*"Redhair"* CROW *enters veranda* R., *chased by* HUTTON *and* WINTERS. [WINTERS *uses her parasol as sword.*] *She crosses* D. L.—*they lunge—she runs* R. HART *enters with lantern, stands top step, encouraging the hunters, and* WINTERS *lunges* R. *She avoids them and exits* L. *arch. They follow and bump* ROACH *who is entering arch* L.)

ROACH. Gentlemen, gentlemen . . .

WINTERS and HUTTON. Sorry, sir!

HART. (*Crosses* L. *to* C.) Time for the inspection, sir.

ROACH. (*Crosses to* C.) Yes, Frank. I'm afraid you and I must return to duty. I'm sorry to deprive you of the . . . charms of . . .

HART. Oh, that's alright, sir. Fair shares—someone else's turn this year.

ROACH. Turn?

HART. Well, she's an annual affair, sir.

ROACH. Oh, I see. Well, we'd better begin. We'll start at the east gate and work our way round to the piquets.

... (*Crosses* R. *to* R. *doors and exits.* HART *follows, looking wistfully where girl has exited.*)

(*They leave via veranda. MUSIC swells. LIGHTS change to early morning setting. MUSIC, down to a crossover fade with different melody at slower tempo, indicates passage of time.*)

ACT ONE

Scene 5

The Mess. The ball. Early morning. As MUSIC and LIGHTS change, loving couples enter U. L. *onto veranda and exit* R. *doors.* TRULY *with blue-dressed* CROW, BOULTON *and yellow-dress follow. As they exit,* PRADAH *enters* L. *arch, straightens bottles* D. L. COLONEL *enters* C. *veranda from* U. L. *after lovers. As he crosses* D. R. *to his chair* PRADAH *sees him.*

PRADAH. May I fetch anything for you, Colonel sahib?
COLONEL. (*Sits.*) No. No, thank you, Pradah Singh. I am in need of a new pair of legs. (*Sinks deep into chair.*)
PRADAH. (*Crosses to* C.) I shall endeavour to see that you are not disturbed, Colonel.
COLONEL. Thank you, Pradah Singh.

(PRADAH SINGH *goes to watch from veranda. The* COLONEL'S *eyes close. Silence.* MEM STRANG *comes onto veranda from* R., *murmurs with* PRADAH SINGH, *who indicates* COLONEL. *She smiles, he bows and goes off* L. *She crosses* D. R. C., *smiling at her husband. She stands by him.*)

MEM. (*Crosses* D. R. *to* COLONEL.) I thought you were feeling a little tired, Colonel dear.
COLONEL. Oh, Mem ... (*Struggles to rise.*)

MEM. No, no, don't get up.

COLONEL. (*Sinks back.*) If you will forgive me, my dear. (*They hold hands briefly.*)

MEM. I'd forgive you anything. (*Her hand on his. Pause.*) You know, it's been a lovely ball.

COLONEL. Has it, Mem?

MEM. (*Looks at him.*) Why, yes.

COLONEL. . . . It's something one feels—one owes to the Past.

MEM. I know. (*A pause.*) Colonel, dear?

COLONEL. Um?

MEM. Would you do something for me?

COLONEL. What?

MEM. Well, I've spent all evening dancing with bounding young men and doddering old bores. (*Rises.*) I should so like to dance with my own dear husband.

COLONEL. Oh, dear. Must I?

MEM. It's an order.

COLONEL. Very well. (*Rises, smiling, extends arm.* OFFSTAGE: *Curious sound—a muffled cry.*) What on earth was that? (*Steps back* D. R.)

MEM. What, dear?

COLONEL. Extraordinary. (*They dance again.*) Thought I heard . . . Come along, Mem!

MEM. Thank you, Colonel, dear. (OFFSTAGE: *A deep scream of pain and terror.* MEM *runs* U. *to* R. C. *pillar, followed by* COLONEL.) It's Marjorie . . . !

MRS. HASSELTINE. (*Off.*) Help . . . ! Help me! Help me!

(MEM *runs.*)

WINTERS. (*Off.*) What the devil was that?!

COLONEL. Pradah Singh!

(PRADAH *enters* D. L. *onto veranda and to* L. *of* MRS. HASSELTINE. TRULY *from* D. L. *to veranda* U. L. *of* MRS. HASSELTINE. FOTHERGILL D. L. *to* L. C. *table* WINTERS *from* U. R. *to* U. R. *of* MRS. HASSELTINE.

BOULTON U. R. *to between* TRULY *and* WINTERS.
MEM *is still short of veranda as* MRS. HASSELTINE
*scrabbles on all fours onto veranda—moving at a
terrifying pace—making mindless noises—hair di-
shevelled, dress torn—coming from* R.)

MRS. HASSELTINE. Ah . . . ! Ah . . . ! Ah . . . !

(PRADAH SINGH *runs to her from veranda* L., *crouches,
trying to lift her.* MEM *has reached her.* WINTERS
and BOULTON *run on from* L. *So does* DRAKE. *The
MUSIC breaks off raggedly.*)

MEM. My dear! What's happened?! (MRS. HASSEL-
TINE *clings to her.*)
MRS. HASSELTINE. Mem . . . ! Mem . . . !
MEM. (*Rocks her.*) It's alright, it's alright, it's al-
right. . . .

(MRS. HASSELTINE *is in total terror. The others mutter
stupid things: "What's happened?", etc.*)

COLONEL. Pradah Singh—brandy. Quickly. (PRADAH
crosses D. L. *table with brandy.* TRULY *from* L. C. *to* L.
of MRS. HASSELTINE, *helps her up.* WINTERS *from* U. R.
to R. *of* MRS. HASSELTINE, *helps her up.*)
PRADAH. Yes, Colonel.

(WIMBORNE, V.C., *runs on from veranda,* L. WIMBORNE,
from U. L., *pushes* TRULY *away.* TRULY *crosses* D.
toward PRADAH. ADJUTANT *from* L. C. *to* L. *of* WIM-
BORNE. BOULTON *from* U. R. *to* R. *of* WINTERS. AD-
JUTANT *tells* BOULTON *to get* DOCTOR, *crosses* D. *to*
PRADAH. BOULTON *to* L. *of* U. *veranda steps, calls*
DOCTOR. HUTTON *enters* R. *doors.* FOTHERGILL, *arch*
L.)

WIMBORNE. What the devil's happened?!

(HUTTON *comes after* WIMBORNE, *and* SENIOR SUB-
ALTERN *comes from* D. L. *The* DOCTOR *comes from behind* HART.)

BOULTON. It's Mrs. Hasseltine. She's . . .

(COLONEL *crosses* D. *toward* R. C. *chair.* HUTTON *shouts to* FOTHERGILL *to move* R. C. *table to* R. HUTTON *starts to move* COLONEL'S *chair, but* COLONEL *shoves* R. C. *chair forward.* FOTHERGILL *moves table* D. R. *and joins* HUTTON D. *and meanwhile* WIMBORNE *and* WINTERS *support* MRS. HASSELTINE *and follow* MEM *to* R. C. *chair.* ROACH *enters* L. *arch, crosses to* AD-
JUTANT *and* TRULY. *As* MRS. HASSELTINE *clears veranda* HART *enters* U. R., *crosses* D. *to group* D. L. BOULTON *follows* WIMBORNE, WINTERS *and* MRS. HASSELTINE D. DRAKE *enters doors* R. *to stand with* BOULTON U. *of* R. C. *chair.* WINTERS *joins* DRAKE *and* BOULTON, *having seated* MRS. HASSELTINE.)

COLONEL. Let's get her to a chair, shall we?
MEM. Give me a hand, will you, Alastair—lift her.
WINTERS. She's been attacked. . . .

(ADJUTANT *arrives at veranda, the* SECOND IN COMMAND *from* D. L.)

COLONEL. Over here . . .

(TRULY *comes onto veranda.* WIMBORNE *lifts* MRS. HAS-
SELTINE, *who clings to him, carries her to chair angled towards veranda.* MEM *at his side.*)

MRS. HASSELTINE. Alastair . . . |
ROACH. What's happened?   } (*Together.*)
WIMBORNE. It's alright, Marge, it's
alright. . . .

(*The others are grouping round.* DOCTOR *enters* U. L.

veranda, pushes through DRAKE, BOULTON *and* WINTERS *to* L. *of* MRS. HASSELTINE. *Then* HART *crosses* U. *to join* BOULTON. WAITERS *are against wall, frightened.*)

DOCTOR. Let me through, please, gentlemen. . . .
COLONEL. Let the Doctor through, gentlemen. . . .

(PRADAH SINGH *gives brandy to* MEM *as they lay* MRS. HASSELTINE *back in chair. As* MRS. HASSELTINE *sits* PRADAH *crosses to* MEM, *gives her brandy, then crosses* D. R., *ad libs with* HUTTON *and* FOTHERGILL.)

PRADAH. Brandy, Mem sahib . . .
MEM. Thank you. (*Cradling* MRS. HASSELTINE.) Drink this, dear . . .
DOCTOR. (*Crouches.*) What on earth has happened, Mem?
MEM. She's been attacked, Doctor. . . .

(MILLINGTON *now appears on the empty veranda from* U. L., *rubbing his head behind the ear. He looks bemused, slightly drunk. Crosses* D. L. *of* C.)

DOCTOR. (*Kneels* L. *of* MRS. HASSELTINE, *takes hand and starts examination.*) Let me see, my dear. . . . Let me just see. . . .
WIMBORNE. Who by? That's what I want to know! Who did it?!

(MRS. HASSELTINE, *looking about wildly, suddenly points at* MILLINGTON.)

MRS. HASSELTINE. (*Tears hand from* DOCTOR *and points at* MILLINGTON.) It was him! It was him!
MILLINGTON. (*Vaguely.*) What . . . ?

(WIMBORNE *makes for him.*)

WIMBORNE. (*Grabs* R. *arm with* L. *hand.*) My God, you little . . . ! (WIMBORNE *throws* MILLINGTON D.)

COLONEL. Alastair! (*They freeze at his tone. He turns formally to the* SECOND IN COMMAND.) Major Roach. This officer is under arrest.

ROACH. Mr. Harper, detail two officers.

ADJUTANT. Sir. Mister Fothergill, Mister Hutton. (HUTTON *and* SENIOR SUBALTERN *advance on* MILLINGTON, *who smiles.* . . . FOTHERGILL *to* L., HUTTON *to* R. *of* MILLINGTON.)

CURTAIN

ACT TWO

Scene 1

The Mess. The next evening. The SENIOR SUBALTERN, HUTTON, WINTERS, BOULTON, TRULY *and—rather apart—*DRAKE, *are waiting subdued. Silence. After a moment,* BOULTON *crosses to* WINTERS.

BOULTON. (*Murmurs, crosses* U. *to veranda, looks off.*) ... What do you think they'll do? (*Crosses* D. C. *below veranda.*)
WINTERS. (*Shrugs.*) Court Martial, I should imagine.
BOULTON. (*Turns away.*) Well, he bloody well deserves it.
SENIOR SUBALTERN. ... There is another possibility.
WINTERS. (*Turns back to* COLONEL'S *chair.*) What?
SENIOR SUBALTERN. The Adjutant may convene a Subalterns' court.
TRULY. What's that?
SENIOR SUBALTERN. (*Rises.*) Well, there hasn't been one for some time ... (*Sees* ADJUTANT *enter* R. *doors.*) Attention, gentlemen! (*They rise to attention.* ADJUTANT *enters, crosses* D. *to* R. C. *Pause.*)
ADJUTANT. Good evening.
ALL. Good evening, sir.
ADJUTANT. Be seated, gentlemen. (*Goes* U. *They sit as they were,* WINTERS *on arm of* COLONEL'S *chair. He waits for complete silence. Then he turns, crosses* U. R. C.) This matter is to be settled by Subalterns' Court Martial. I shall explain to you in a moment exactly what that entails. Suffice it to say that—fortunately for us— (*Crosses to* L. *of* C.) Mrs. Hasseltine is agreeable that the matter should remain within the confines of this Regiment.

Provided it is dealt with by us. Which it will be. Mister Fothergill.

SENIOR SUBALTERN. (*Rises.*) Sir.

ADJUTANT. Bring in the accused officer.

SENIOR SUBALTERN. Sir. (SENIOR SUBALTERN *goes off* L. ADJUTANT *taps* C. *chair with crop.* TRULY *moves it* D. L. *of* C. *as* ADJUTANT *crosses* D. R., *then resumes place. Silence. Returns with* MILLINGTON, *who enters first, crosses* R. *to accused's chair.*)

MILLINGTON. Thank you, my dear fellow.

SENIOR SUBALTERN. The accused officer, sir.

ADJUTANT. Sit down, Mister Millington. (MILLINGTON *sits,* SENIOR SUBALTERN *returns to place.*) You are to be tried by Subalterns' (*Crosses* U. C.) Court Martial. I shall now explain that. (*Goes up, turns.*) A Subalterns' Court consists of five officers. (R. *of* C.) One president and four members. There will also be one officer prosecuting, and one defending. Verdict will be by vote of the five. (*A pause.*) A Subalterns' Court Martial has no official existence, gentlemen. It is outside the normal structure of discipline and command. Should a senior officer become officially aware of it, he would be obliged to end it. However, make no mistake. The powers of this court are summary and absolute. There is no appeal to higher authority. Do I make myself plain? (*General murmurs:* "*Yes, sir.*") Now— (*Crosses* U. C.) As to witnesses. You may, by tradition, require any officer (*Crosses* D. C.) of whatever rank to appear before you. You may also call civilian personnel. But should you choose to call a senior officer, gentlemen, his appearance before this court will in no sense affect his official knowledge of these proceedings, which do not exist. Do you understand me? (*Murmured acknowledgment.* [ALL: *Suh!*] MILLINGTON *shakes head, amused chuckle at this doubletalk.* ADJUTANT *turns to* MILLINGTON. *Points to each as named.* MILLINGTON *looks round at them* L.) I do not think you will find this amusing for long, Mister Millington. (*Crosses* U. C.) The Court will convene in this anteroom at midnight tonight.

And on whatever (*Crosses* D. C.) subsequent nights may be required to arrive at a verdict. Pradah Singh will be on duty. But you will neither acknowledge nor address him. The Court will be composed as follows: The president, myself. The members, Mister Boulton, Mister Hart, Mister Winters and Mister Truly. The prosecuting officer will be Mister Fothergill. (*Crosses* D. L. *to* FOTHERGILL *who nods smugly.*) The defending officer, subject to the accused officer's (*Bows to* MILLINGTON.) approval, will be Mister Drake. Are there any questions?

(MILLINGTON *looks amused at shocked* DRAKE.)

MILLINGTON. Am I to understand that I have some option in the matter?
ADJUTANT. Stand up, Mister Millington. (*A moment, then* MILLINGTON *rises, faces* ADJUTANT.) You are entitled, if you wish, to select some other officer to defend you.
MILLINGTON. (*Smiles.*) . . . I suppose I couldn't choose the Colonel? (*General bad taste reaction. Silence.*) Well. Then I am content with Mister Drake. (*Sits.*) He is a gentleman of honour.
ADJUTANT. That is praise indeed. Are there any further questions? (*Crosses to* R. C. *table.*)
DRAKE. (*Rises, hesitant.*) Sir . . .
ADJUTANT. Mister Drake?
DRAKE. Am I . . . obliged to accept this duty?
ADJUTANT. (*Looks at* MILLINGTON.) . . . Mister Millington has chosen you, Mister Drake.
DRAKE. . . . Yes, sir. (*Sits again.*)
ADJUTANT. (*Crosses* C. *two steps.*) Very well! You will now return to your duties, gentlemen. You, Mister Drake, will remain here. Mister Millington will wait outside under escort. Mr. Hutton . . .

(TRULY, WINTERS *exit* R. *doors.* TRULY *closes them.*
HART, HUTTON, MILLINGTON, BOULTON *exit* L. *arch.*

FOTHERGILL *and* DRAKE *exchange bows.* FOTHERGILL *exits* L. *arch.*)

ADJUTANT. (*Crosses to* U. L. *of* R. C. *table.*) I appreciate that you have been under something of a disadvantage since you arrived here, Mister Drake. But it is necessary that Mister Millington be defended. Traditional forms must be observed.

DRAKE. . . . It is simply that I am anxious to do well here, sir.

ADJUTANT. Of course. But there are many ways in which one may serve the Regiment. I don't think you need fear to find yourself guilty by association.

DRAKE. It was wrong of me to raise the matter, sir.

ADJUTANT. (*Crosses* D. *level with* DRAKE.) Not at all. Any young subaltern would appreciate your dilemma. Though I don't think that, in this particular instance, you will need to embarrass yourself unduly. It is very much a fait accompli, is it not?

DRAKE. Still, it is, of course, my duty to defend Mister Millington in the best manner that I can. I see that now, sir.

ADJUTANT. Naturally you will be required to find whatever you can to say in his favour.

DRAKE. No, I mean to say, it is a matter of honour, is it not, sir? The honour of the Regiment demands that Mister Millington be properly defended.

ADJUTANT. . . . As I say, it is necessary to go through the motions. (*Crosses* U. L. *of* R. C. *table.*) But there. You are no fool, Mister Drake. You know what is required of you. (*Crosses* U. R. *of* C.)

DRAKE. . . . To be fair, sir.

ADJUTANT. (*Crosses* R. *to doors.*) Just so. To be fair. To the Regiment. Good. Excellent. Carry on, Mister Drake. (*Exits* R. *doors.* DRAKE *frowns: a moment of unease. The arrival of* MILLINGTON *hardens him.*)

MILLINGTON. (*Enters* L. *to* L. *of* C. *chair.*) Can I come in now, my dear chap . . . ? (*Dry: amused.*) I do hope he persuaded you to take on my case, Arthur.

DRAKE. You are determined to make life impossible for me here, aren't you?

MILLINGTON. For myself, my dear fellow. Not for you.

DRAKE. (*Sits D. R. chair.*) I pray God you have at last succeeded.

MILLINGTON. (*Crosses R. to C.*) Amen to that, old man. (*Pause.*)

DRAKE. I don't know how you can expect me to defend you. I've no sympathy for you whatever.

MILLINGTON. I understand that isn't necessary.

DRAKE. I know nothing of courtroom procedure.

MILLINGTON. (*Crosses to R. C. chair.*) For this particular charade, I doubt you'll need to.

DRAKE. You'll get a fair trial, Millington! A damned sight fairer than you deserve!

MILLINGTON. (*Sits R. C. chair.*) My dear Arthur. With you to defend me, how can I fail?

DRAKE. (*Pause. Crosses L. to L. C. chair.*) . . . You had better tell me what happened.

MILLINGTON. I wouldn't want to shock you, Arthur.

DRAKE. (*Picks up chair.*) For God's sake!

MILLINGTON. I, ah, endeavoured to touch her.

DRAKE. (*Crosses to original R. C. chair marks with chair. Starts to place.*) Where?

MILLINGTON. (*Grins.*) In the shrubbery.

DRAKE. (*Jerks chair up again. Furious.*) Now look, Millington . . . !

MILLINGTON. My dear fellow . . . ?

DRAKE. (*Puts chair down and sits. Controls himself.*) . . . Just tell me what happened.

MILLINGTON. . . . There's little enough to tell, Arthur. I am, as you know, anxious to absent myself. When I saw Mrs. Hasseltine go into the Folly, it seemed an admirable opportunity to, ah—if you'll pardon the expression—to combine business with pleasure. So I . . .

ah . . . endeavoured to come to grips with her. Without, it must be admitted, any marked success.

DRAKE. You forget, Millington, I saw Mrs. Hasseltine when she came into the Mess.

MILLINGTON. My dear fellow, I saw her before she went into the Mess. She was quite unimpaired, I assure you.

DRAKE. Her dress was torn. She was in a state of hysteria.

MILLINGTON. Perhaps she tore it on the shrubbery. (*Crosses* D. *below* COLONEL'*s chair*.) Does it really matter?

DRAKE. (*Rises*.) Exactly how much of this assault can you remember?

MILLINGTON. My dear Arthur, it was an assault only in the most technical sense.

DRAKE. You were drunk, weren't you?

MILLINGTON. Not that drunk. (*Crosses* L. *of* C.)

DRAKE. (*Turns to him*.) Enough to have no clear recollection of what occurred.

MILLINGTON. (*Crosses to* L. C.) My dear fellow, I'm never that drunk. You've seen what happens when I drink too much. (*Turns to* DRAKE *who has eased* D. *behind him*.) I go down like a felled ox. There's nothing for me between clarity and oblivion.

DRAKE. If you are to be believed. (*Crosses* D. R.)

MILLINGTON. In heaven's name, what does it matter? I'm guilty, Arthur. I admit it!

DRAKE. I doubt you'll be permitted to in the courtroom.

MILLINGTON. Whyever not?

DRAKE. You'll be obliged to plead not guilty. That is customary to ensure a fair trial.

MILLINGTON. (*Steps down*.) By all means let us plead not guilty, but let us have an end to the matter as rapidly as we may. (*Pause*.)

DRAKE. (*Filled with contempt*.) You are very proud of yourself, aren't you, Millington?

MILLINGTON. . . . It was necessary.

DRAKE. (*Crosses to meet him* D. C.) Necessary. To assault an older woman, simply in order to—

MILLINGTON. In heaven's name, anyone would think I'd raped the blasted female.

DRAKE. Didn't you?

MILLINGTON. (*Demonstrates with* DRAKE'S R. *arm.*) My dear Arthur, I took hold of her arm, she pulled away, I took hold of it again—and wallop! She did me more damage than I did her.

DRAKE. How so?

MILLINGTON. Well, look, my dear fellow. (*Pulls forward right ear.*) I've a gash that must be every bit of what—two inches long.

DRAKE. . . . That is the work of Mrs. Hasseltine?

MILLINGTON. (*Faces* DRAKE.) It certainly isn't the work of myself.

DRAKE. How did she do it?

MILLINGTON. She hit me, Arthur.

DRAKE. With what?

MILLINGTON. I haven't the faintest idea. (*Crosses* L. *to* D. L. *table.*) It felt at the time like the Cawnpore cannon. Laid me out cold.

DRAKE. I see. And that was for touching her on the arm?

MILLINGTON. My dear Arthur—

DRAKE. (*Disgusted.*) You're lying, Millington.

MILLINGTON. (*Crosses* U. *to* L. C. *table.*) Well, if you wish to believe me guilty of having raped her up hill and down dale, it really doesn't make any difference, does it?

DRAKE. (*Crosses to* R. *of* MILLINGTON.) And those are the grounds on which I am to defend you, are they? That in fact you did nothing?

MILLINGTON. (*Smiles.*) . . . Are you sure you have properly understood the Adjutant's instructions, Arthur? Those are the grounds on which you are to fail to defend me.

DRAKE. (*Crosses* D. R. *of* C.) Oh yes. You would like to believe that, wouldn't you?

MILLINGTON. (*Follows.*) I am easily satisfied, Ar—

DRAKE. (*Crosses to* MILLINGTON.) Well, you'll get a fair trial, Millington! I shall see to that! Much as I should prefer to prosecute you, I shall defend you to the utmost of my ability! For I, at least, have some conception of where my duty lies! (*Turns away, crosses* U. *to* R. *steps.*) However repugnant that duty may be to me.

MILLINGTON. (*Crosses to* L. *of him.*) . . . You . . . ah . . . you won't exceed requirements, will you, Arthur? You know, you could do yourself a great deal of good here . . .

DRAKE. (*Turns.*) Get out of here. You make me sick.

MILLINGTON. (*Crosses towards arch.*) Well, no matter. I fancy you will find there is little you can do for this particular lost cause. Au revoir, my dear fellow. See you at the witching hour. (MILLINGTON *goes.* DRAKE, *alone, is angry, uncertain. He marches off veranda* R.)

(*As the* LIGHTS FADE, *and come up to night setting: At* PRADAH SINGH'S *direction, the* WAITERS *bring on lamps, arrange furniture for the courtroom. Upstage, long table, five chairs. Stage* R., *prosecution table and chair. Stage* L., *defence table and chairs* [*two*]. *Stage* C., *witness chair.*)

ACT TWO

SCENE 2

The Mess. Midnight. The trial. PRADAH SINGH *claps hands*, WAITERS *run off* R. DRAKE *enters with sheets of paper, looks at furniture as* MILLINGTON *comes on.* PRADAH SINGH *bows, turns to leave.*

MILLINGTON. (*Enters* L. *arch, crosses to* PRADAH.

PRADAH *facing* U. *at* C. *of table* [*court*], *when* MILLINGTON *speaks he turns front at attention*.) Good evening, Pradah Singh. (*Turns front.*) Oh!

DRAKE. (*Enters* R. *doors, crosses to* R. *of court table.*) Pradah Singh.

MILLINGTON. Ssshh! (PRADAH SINGH *turns back.*)

DRAKE. I . . . understand that I am not to address you. But . . . could you tell me please where we sit? (*Very nervous.*)

PRADAH. (*Indicates.*) The Defence is seated over there, sahib. (*Points to* D. L. *table. Starts* U., R. *of court table.*)

DRAKE. . . . Thank you. (*Crosses* L. *of* C., *turns to* PRADAH *who stops and turns back.*)

PRADAH. (*Sympathy: indicates.*) The Court, sahib. The Witness. The Prosecution, sahib.

DRAKE. Thank you, Pradah Singh.

PRADAH. Sahib . . . (*He goes* U. R., *veranda.* MILLINGTON *has sat back, leaning on court table, amused, as soon as he knows where.* DRAKE *puts papers on desk, drops paper, picks up. Wanders about, clearly very nervous. Sits chair* R. *of* D. L. *table.*)

MILLINGTON. (*Amused.*) You appear nervous, Arthur. (*Crosses* R. *below* COLONEL'S *chair. No reply.*) Well, you are on trial, too. Are you not? (DRAKE *ignores him, sits at desk, checks top sheet, scribbles.*) What are you doing, my dear fellow?

DRAKE. I am endeavouring to find some points to make in your favour.

MILLINGTON. (*Crosses* L. *to* DRAKE.) Oh, do let me see. (*Leans forward: reads.*) "One, drink. Two, size." Size of what, Arthur? "Three . . . Character of Mrs. Hasseltine, question mark." I think I'd forgo that one, if I were you. "Four . . ." Oh, dear. No four? Is that the sum of my virtues, Arthur?

(HUTTON *comes on, doors* R., *stands* U. *on top step by his chair.*)

HUTTON. Stand up!

ACT II   CONDUCT UNBECOMING   63

(*They rise,* MILLINGTON *slowly. The Members of the Court file on,* TRULY *first.* ADJUTANT *last.* MILLINGTON *amused at their solemnity. Eventually they stand behind their chairs. At* U. *table:* HARPER C.; HART, *then* WINTERS *to his right.* BOULTON, *then* TRULY *to his left.* SENIOR SUBALTERN *goes to Prosecution desk. A silence.*)

ADJUTANT. Be seated, gentlemen. (*They do. He sits last.* HUTTON *closes doors.*) This court is now in session. Mister Millington, rise. (*With a longsuffering look for* DRAKE, *he does.*) Mister Hart.

HART. (*Rises.*) Mister President. The charge before this court reads as follows: (ADJUTANT *and* FOTHERGILL *follow charge on own copies. Reads from sheet.*) "That on the seventeenth instant, the accused officer, Second Lieutenant Millington, E, serving with this Regiment, did attack, wound and assault Mrs. Marjorie Hasseltine, then a guest of this Regiment, the widow of the late Major Robert Hasseltine, also of this Regiment. That in this, as in his prior actions, he has grossly insulted his brother officers, he has betrayed the trust reposed in him by his Colonel and his brother officers, he has brought the name of this Regiment into dishonour and disrepute, and he has conducted himself in a manner unbecoming an officer and a gentleman." The charge ends, Mister President. (*Sits.*)

ADJUTANT. How do you plead, Mister Millington? Guilty or not guilty?

MILLINGTON. Indifferent, Mister President.

DRAKE. (*Rises quickly.*) The accused officer pleads not guilty, Mister President.

ADJUTANT. . . . Not guilty, Mister Drake?

DRAKE. . . . Well, yes, Mister President. (FOTHERGILL *reacts, drops charges on table.* HART *and* BOULTON *exchange surprise, others react.*)

ADJUTANT. I see. You, Mister Millington, will remain

silent, or these proceedings will be continued in your absence. Do you understand me?

MILLINGTON. Yes, Mister President.

ADJUTANT. Sit down. (MILLINGTON *sits.*) Both of you. (DRAKE *sits.*) Mister Fothergill.

SENIOR SUBALTERN. (*Rises smartly.*) I am ready to call my first witness, Mister President.

ADJUTANT. Carry on.

SENIOR SUBALTERN. I call the Doctor. (*Sits.*)

ADJUTANT. Mister Hutton. (HUTTON *rises,* ["sir,"] *goes* L., *opens* U. *door* R., *returns with* DOCTOR.)

HUTTON. Would you come in, please, sir.

DOCTOR. Of course. (*Enters, crosses* L. *to* R. *side of court table.*) Mister President. (*Clicks heels.*)

ADJUTANT. (*Rises.*) Be seated, Doctor, please.

DOCTOR. Thank you. (*Sits in witness chair.* HUTTON *closes door and sits.*)

ADJUTANT. (*Smiles.*) I am obliged to remind you, sir, that you are on your honour to speak the truth.

DOCTOR. Of course, Mister President.

ADJUTANT. Thank you, sir. Mister Fothergill.

SENIOR SUBALTERN. (*Comes from desk. Crosses to* R. *of witness chair.*) Doctor, (*Clicks, bows.*) on the night of the seventeenth a ball took place which was interrupted by . . . a most unfortunate incident. (*Looks at* MILLINGTON.) Did you examine Mrs. Hasseltine later at the hospital, Doctor?

DOCTOR. I did indeed, yes.

SENIOR SUBALTERN. Had she been attacked?

DOCTOR. Most certainly. There is no question of that.

SENIOR SUBALTERN. In a serious manner, Doctor?

DOCTOR. In my opinion it was a most gross and cowardly assault.

SENIOR SUBALTERN. (*Crosses above to* L. *of chair.*) I see. And did Mrs. Hasseltine give any indication, in your presence, of who might have been responsible?

DOCTOR. She did, yes. She made a direct accusation.

SENIOR SUBALTERN. Against whom, sir?

DOCTOR. (HART *glances at* MILLINGTON.) Against Mr. Millington. I pointed out that it was an extremely serious charge to bring against a young officer. (WINTERS *and* HART *make notes.*)

SENIOR SUBALTERN. But she repeated the charge?

DOCTOR. She did, yes. Most emphatically.

SENIOR SUBALTERN. Thank you, Doctor. (*Crosses* D. R. *of* DOCTOR. *Looks at Court.*) Finally I should like to ask whether—when you examined Mister Millington, as I believe you did this morning—

DOCTOR. Yes, I did.

SENIOR SUBALTERN —whether you found anything to indicate that he might have been responsible for this attack?

DOCTOR. You are referring to the gash on his head?

SENIOR SUBALTERN. I am, yes.

DOCTOR. Well, Mister Millington himself admitted to me that it was Mrs. Hasseltine who had struck him. (HART *leans forward.*)

SENIOR SUBALTERN. Struck him when, Doctor?

DOCTOR. As I understand it, during the course of a struggle.

SENIOR SUBALTERN. (*Looks at* MILLINGTON.) Are you saying that Mister Millington *admitted* to you that he had attacked Mrs. Hasseltine?

DOCTOR. So far as I am aware, he has freely admitted that to anyone who has asked him.

(*All look at* MILLINGTON. MILLINGTON *nods agreeably to* FOTHERGILL, *then to Court.* HART *makes note, tears sheet off and hands to* ADJUTANT. WINTERS *and* TRULY *make notes.*)

SENIOR SUBALTERN. (*Pleased surprise.*) I see. (*Looks at Court.*) Thank you, Doctor. (*Returns to place, sits.*)

ADJUTANT. Mister Drake?

DRAKE. (*Rises. Best manners, nervous. Anxious to do what he imagines is required of him. Hesitant.*) Mister President . . . Gentlemen of the Court . . . Doctor . . .

Doctor. Mister Drake . . .

Drake. Doctor . . . I am not clear . . . in my own mind . . . exactly what Mrs. Hasseltine's injuries amount to. (Hart *looks at* Winters *behind* Adjutant.)

Doctor. Well . . . She was bruised about the wrists and arms. (Fothergill *fiddles with pencil.*) The palms of her hands were skinned. The legs also, down here. (*Shins.*) The knees were bruised. She was otherwise cut about the body. Her dress was torn . . . (*Moved by the outrage.*)

Drake. . . . Would it be fair to say that . . . many of these injuries might have been sustained in . . . running through the trees and shrubbery that surround the Folly?

Doctor. I think it would be fair to say that, yes. However, it must be added that she was only running because she had been attacked.

Adjutant. (*Quick in.*) Just so, Mister Drake.

Drake. Yes, Mister President. Had she been . . . in any other sense . . . interfered with, Doctor? (Fothergill *and others are shocked.* Truly *and* Winters *exchange looks.*)

Doctor. Do you mean *sexually?*

Adjutant. Mister Drake. Mister Millington is not charged with rape, but with assault.

Drake. Yes, Mister President.

Adjutant. Very well. (*Dismissive.*) The Court does not require an answer to that question, Doctor.

Doctor. Mister President.

Drake. (*At a loss.*) . . . Well, would it be fair to say, sir, that this was . . . relatively speaking . . . an unsuccessful attack? (Fothergill *is startled. Big reaction by all.*)

Adjutant. (*Very quickly in.*) Mister Drake, it is of no concern to this Court whether Mister Millington succeeded or failed in what he intended to do. It is the attempt with which he is charged.

Drake. . . . I was merely trying to suggest, Mister

President, that there might be some mitigation in the fact that he failed.

DOCTOR. But he did not fail, Mister Drake. One cannot measure the effects of an assault of this kind purely in physical terms.

ADJUTANT. Exactly so, Doctor.

DOCTOR. The shock to the *nervous* system—to the *emotions* of the patient is *extreme*. You saw for yourself, Mister Drake. Mrs. Hasseltine was in a state of terror—bordering, in my opinion, on acute hysteria. (BOULTON *and* HART *make notes,* TRULY *looks at* MILLINGTON.)

ADJUTANT. (*Quickly in.*) The Court finds no mitigation in the circumstances you describe, Mister Drake.

DRAKE. No, Mister President. (*Pause.*) But I am not clear, Doctor . . . as to exactly why . . . Mrs. Hasseltine was so afraid. (*Impatient reaction,* HART *sighs.*)

DOCTOR. I cannot believe that is a serious comment, Mister Drake.

DRAKE. I mean to say, Mister Millington is not a large man, sir. On the day that you examined us, you said that you would have to "put some meat on him." (HART *looks at* ADJUTANT.)

ADJUTANT. (*Quickly in.*) We appear to have strayed yet again from the purpose of these proceedings, Mister Drake.

DRAKE. Well, it is surely relevant, Mister President, that Mister Millington is hardly capable of any . . . serious assault (*Big reaction.* HART *and* BOULTON *shift in chair.* WINTERS *and* TRULY *react.* FOTHERGILL *throws down pencil.*) on Mrs. Hasseltine, particularly if he was affected by alcohol at the time. . . .

(MILLINGTON *is attentive now.*)

DOCTOR. It is surely well known that a man may find many times his strength in the bottle?

DRAKE. But—Doctor . . .

ADJUTANT. (*Quickly in.*) Mister Drake. This Court

will not accept drunkenness as mitigation of any act on the part of Mister Millington.

DRAKE. But does it not . . . to some extent . . . reduce his responsibility, Mister President?

ADJUTANT. (*Quickly in.*) I do not think so. The responsibility for drinking to excess remains his alone.

DOCTOR. I hardly think, Mister Drake, that this is a line you would do well to pursue. (*All turn to* DRAKE.)

ADJUTANT. Just so, Mister Drake. (*Mounting acid.*) Well, Mister Drake, have you any further questions for this witness?

(*Against a wall,* DRAKE *goes to pick up his notes. He has one point left.* MILLINGTON *noticeably relaxes* . . . DRAKE *hesitates, uncertain.* . . . *Looks at notes.*)

MILLINGTON. Honestly— (*Helpful. Murmurs.*) I'd let it *drop*, if I were you. The cards are against you.

ADJUTANT. Mister Millington. You will not be warned again. (*Pause.* DRAKE *glares at* MILLINGTON. *Small pause.*) Well, Mister Drake, we are waiting.

DRAKE. (*Glares at* MILLINGTON: *turns.*) Doctor. Would you not expect a woman of Mrs. Hasseltine's character (*All big reaction,* FOTHERGILL *outraged.*) to be able easily to deal with the importunate advances—

(MILLINGTON *covers his eyes at this folly.*)

ADJUTANT. (*Climactically.*) *No,* Mister Drake! We are not here to discuss the *character* of Mrs. Hasseltine, but the *actions* of Mister Millington.

DRAKE. But it is surely relevant, Mister Pres—

ADJUTANT. *No,* Mister Drake! It is not relevant! You will not refer to the matter again.

DRAKE. . . . But, Mister President. On the very day that we arrived here, Mister Fothergill (FOTHERGILL *leans forward as if to stop him. Others look at* FOTHER-) GILL.) issued a warning in the most specific terms as to the character of Mrs. . . .

ADJUTANT. (*Quickly in.*) It is of *no* concern to this Court what the Senior Subaltern may or may not have chosen to say to you on a private occasion! So far as this Court is concerned, Mrs. Hasseltine is a woman of the highest character and probity. Do you understand me?

DRAKE. (*Painful dilemma.*) . . . I do not know how I am to defend this officer, if you will allow me no "latitude" in the matter of—!

ADJUTANT. (*Very quickly in.*) You are entitled to whatever (*Sarcastically.*) "*latitude*" I choose to give you as President of this Court and no more! Now. Have I made myself quite plain, Mister Drake?

DRAKE. (*Turns away: quietly. Turns front.*) . . . Yes, Mister President. You have indeed.

ADJUTANT. Very well. You will confine yourself to questions that are proper to this enquiry.

MILLINGTON. For God's sake, sit down—you're embarrassing us all.

ADJUTANT. Mr. Millington, you have interrupted these proceedings for the last time.

DRAKE. Doctor, when Mr. Millington passed out at the Mess Night, did you not say that "gentlemen who cannot hold their liquor should not drink"? (*Reaction*, HART *shifts*, FOTHERGILL *exasperated.*)

DOCTOR. I may have said that, yes.

ADJUTANT. I have already told you, Mr. Drake . . .

DRAKE. Well surely, on the evidence, Mr. Millington is made not stronger, but weaker by alcohol? (BOULTON *looks at* ADJUTANT.)

DOCTOR. Mr. Drake, since you persist in pursuing this matter, I am forced to tell you that in my opinion Mr. Millington is on the point of becoming a complete and incurable drunkard. (*All look at* MILLINGTON.) It is almost certain therefore that there would be periods when he would have no control whatsoever over his actions.

DRAKE. (*To* MILLINGTON: *stunned.*) . . . Is this true?

MILLINGTON. Don't sound so shocked, for Christ's sake. (*There is a strange, taut, overstrung mixture of amusement, contempt—almost sub-hysteria in* MILLINGTON *at this point.*)

ADJUTANT. You will not put questions directly to the accused officer, Mister Drake.

MILLINGTON. He has no idea what is required of him, Mister President. You should have made your instructions plainer!

ADJUTANT. Mister Millington . . .

MILLINGTON. (*Rises.*) You're a fool, (*Bangs table.*) Arthur! You are expected to go through the motions, not to indulge a talent for legalistic moralising!

ADJUTANT. If you continue in this vein, Mister Millington, I shall have you put out at once.

MILLINGTON. (*Rises to attention.*) I should prefer that, Mister President. (*Crosses below table. All look at* DRAKE *with hostility.*)

ADJUTANT. . . . I have every sympathy with your point of view. (DRAKE *sits.*) You are entitled to rejoin your escort if you wish.

MILLINGTON. Thank you, sir. (*Crosses* R. *and* U. *round table to* L. *arch. Stops, turns back.*) What a bourgeois little creature you are, to be sure, Arthur. (*Exits* L.)

(*Pause. Anger directed at* DRAKE.)

ADJUTANT. Mister Drake.

(DRAKE *rises. He is stunned by the attitudes of* HARPER *and* DOCTOR—*a reversal that seems to have made him the guilty party. He stands. Silence.*)

DRAKE. (*Rises. Numbly:*) . . . I have no more questions for this witness. (*Sits.*)

ADJUTANT. Thank you, Mister Drake. (*To* DOCTOR.) I am sorry if these proceedings have proved distasteful for you, sir. Thank you for attending them.

DOCTOR. (*Rises.* HUTTON *opens* R. *doors as* DOCTOR

turns. FOTHERGILL *shuffles papers.*) Mister President. Gentlemen. (*The* DOCTOR *departs.* HUTTON *closes doors, and sits. A pause.*)

ADJUTANT. Mister Fothergill.

SENIOR SUBALTERN. (*Rises, subdued, crosses to* R. *of Court.*) Mister President. The next logical step would be to call Mrs. Hasseltine. I would hope that the defending officer would not find that necessary, but that he would accept a written deposition from her. (*Hands deposition to* TRULY *who hands it to* ADJUTANT. FOTHERGILL *crosses* R. *and sits in his chair.*)

ADJUTANT. Quite so, Mister Fothergill. Mister Drake? (*Pause.*) Mister Drake! (*Hands deposition to* DRAKE *who doesn't take it.*)

DRAKE. (*Rises. Not taking it in.*) . . . I don't know, Mister President. I . . . need to think.

ADJUTANT. . . . Very well. This session is now closed. (*Rises. All rise.*) The Court will reconvene at midnight tomorrow. You will leave this Mess quickly and quietly. (*Gentlemen all "sir!"*) Mister Drake, you will remain here. (HUTTON *opens doors.* TRULY *and* WINTERS *exit* R. *doors, followed by* HUTTON *and* FOTHERGILL. ADJUTANT *follows and closes doors.* HART *and* BOULTON *exit* L. *arch glancing at* DRAKE. DRAKE *turns* D. *to papers on table* D. L. *as* ADJUTANT *closes doors.* HEAD WAITER *and* LAL, *an Indian servant woman, appear on veranda from off* U. L., *see* ADJUTANT *at door and run off* U. R. DRAKE *and* HARPER *are alone.* DRAKE *is still stunned.* ADJUTANT *comes down, crosses to below* C. *of court table.*) Now look here, Drake, just what do you think you're playing at?

DRAKE. . . . I was trying to do my duty . . . as given me by you . . . to defend him, sir.

ADJUTANT. To defend him, yes! Not to cast doubt on the persons and institutions of this Regiment!

DRAKE. . . . He is surely entitled to a fair trial?

ADJUTANT. Do you suggest that he will not receive one from us?

DRAKE. . . . I do not know . . . what it is you require of me.

ADJUTANT. You know very well what is required of you, Mister Drake. You will not play games with me.

DRAKE. . . . I am to "go through the motions." I am to make no serious attempt to defend him.

ADJUTANT. Is there some doubt in your mind as to his guilt?

DRAKE. . . . No. None whatever. . . . (*Almost sounds amused.*)

ADJUTANT. Very well then. Tomorrow you will plead Mister Millington guilty, as clearly he wishes you to. As for yourself, we shall see how you conduct yourself in the weeks to come. You have made an excellent beginning here. I should not like to think we had been mistaken in you, too, Mister Drake.

DRAKE. . . . No, sir.

ADJUTANT. (*Crosses to court table, gets papers.*) Good. (*Tosses sheets onto table.*) Well— Here is Mrs. Hasseltine's deposition. (*Turns to* DRAKE—*who doesn't take it.*) You will be requiring it since you will not be calling her. (DRAKE *slowly takes paper.*) That is all, Mister Drake. (*Starts to go,* R., *up steps.*)

DRAKE. (*Crosses to* L. *end court table. When* ADJUTANT *is at top step:*) . . . Mister Harper.

ADJUTANT. (*His back to* DRAKE.) Well?

DRAKE. . . . Surely Mister Millington is entitled to face his accuser? (*A pause.*)

ADJUTANT. (*Crosses* L. *to* C.) . . . Are you being wilfully obstructive, Mister Drake?

DRAKE. (*One pace to* ADJUTANT.) No, sir, but—

ADJUTANT. Do you not appreciate to what extent we are already indebted to Mrs. Hasseltine? Do you not realize that—had she chosen to make an official charge against him—Mister Millington would now be facing public Court Martial?

DRAKE. But surely—

ADJUTANT. By officers not of this Regiment?! That he would be publicly disgraced! And so should we!

DRAKE. But is his disgrace not inevitable in any event?

ADJUTANT. Why, Mister Drake?

DRAKE. Well, if he's found guilty you will surely be obliged to be rid of him.

ADJUTANT. I do not think so. Mister Millington will find that we have duties for him yet. Of an unpleasant nature, to be sure. But admirably well suited to his condition.

DRAKE. . . . You mean to keep him here?

ADJUTANT. For a year or two, certainly. Five perhaps. Or even ten. The option lies with us, Mister Drake. We must see how long it takes Mr. Millington to find his place with us, and to learn a simple lesson—that this Regiment is not mocked.

DRAKE. . . . I see. (*Turns* L.)

ADJUTANT. (*Crosses* D. *to* R. *of* C.) You can do nothing for Mr. Millington and only harm to yourself. Do you understand?

DRAKE. (*Turns to* ADJUTANT. *Pause: comes to attention.*) . . . I request to be relieved of this duty, sir.

ADJUTANT. . . . No, Mister Drake. You have an admirable opportunity of serving this Regiment. (*Crossing* R. *and out* R. *doors.*) I shall follow your progress with the keenest interest. Good night, Mister Drake. (*Goes.* DRAKE *crosses* L. *to* D. L. *table, drops papers on it. Stares in an agonising dilemma. Suddenly the* INDIAN WAITER *and* LAL *reappear anxiously on* U. R. *veranda, afraid to be caught.*)

WAITER. (*Above her.*) It is that one—be quick. (*Goes to* L. C. *pillar.*)

LAL. (*Crosses* D. *to* R. *end court table.*) Sahib . . . ! Sahib . . . !

DRAKE. (*Turns.*) . . . Yes?

LAL. Ask about the bleeding, sahib . . . !

DRAKE. . . . What?

LAL. The bleeding, sahib! And Mrs. Bandanai . . . !

(PRADAH SINGH *comes on, furious,* R. *doors.* LAL *flees to veranda and off* L. WAITER *goes immediately on* PRADAH'S *entrance.* PRADAH *crosses* U. *to above table and to* L. *of it.*)

PRADAH. What are you doing here?! Be off with you! Chelly jaow, chelly jaow. (*Crosses above table to* L. *of it.*)
DRAKE. (*Crosses* R. *of court table, tries to stop* PRADAH.) No, wait . . . ! (*But she has gone.*)
PRADAH. (*Crosses* D. L. *of court table.*) I am sorry, sahib. It will not happen again, sahib.
DRAKE. . . . Who was that?
PRADAH. The servant of Mem Hasseltine, sahib.
DRAKE. (*Steps to witness chair.*) Mrs. Hasseltine?
PRADAH. Yes, sahib. I shall take the strongest possible—
DRAKE. No. No. (*Pause. Level with* PRADAH.) Who is Mrs. Bandanai, Pradah Singh?
PRADAH. . . . She is the widow of an Indian officer, Jemadar Bandanai, sahib.
DRAKE. Could you . . . arrange for me to speak with her?
PRADAH. (*Embarrassed.*) Well, I . . . I don't know, sahib. It is . . . not usual, sahib. . . .
DRAKE. It is important, Pradah Singh. It will be of assistance to Mr. Millington.
PRADAH. (*Crosses* D. L. *to* L. *table.*) Mr. Millington, sahib . . . ?
DRAKE. Whose father, I know, you greatly admired.
PRADAH. (*Turns to him.*) . . . I will see what I can do, sahib.
DRAKE. Thank you. . . .
PRADAH. Sahib. (*Exits* L. *arch. As he exits,* DRAKE *runs to* D. L. *table, gets papers, then exits* R. *doors, running.* PRADAH SINGH *claps hands.* WAITERS *run on.*)

(*LIGHTS GO DOWN. COME UP. The furniture is still set for the Court. Pause.*)

ACT TWO

Scene 3

The Mess. The trial. The next midnight. MILLINGTON *comes on, arrogant, angry,* R. *doors to* L. *of witness chair and sits. After a pause,* DRAKE *enters. He does not at once see* MILLINGTON. *He crosses the stage. He has taken a small step to being stronger now. Anger has begun: he has found something that puzzles him. He has a card (the* SECOND IN COMMAND).

MILLINGTON. (*Very acid, arrogant.*) Well. My very own St. George. My knight in shining armour. I have come to change my plea, Arthur. (*Crossing* R.) Do you understand me? I am changing my plea to guilty.

DRAKE. . . . I understand you very well.

MILLINGTON. (*Crosses* R. *above witness chair.*) Good. (*Pause.*) Well. (*Acid smile. Crosses* U. L. *of witness chair.*) No argument as to the honour of the Regiment, Arthur? (*Sits.*) No insistence on—what was it you called it?—a fair hearing?

DRAKE. You are very confident, aren't you, Millington?

MILLINGTON. (*Crosses* L. C.) I am confident of what I need to be. I must say I regard (*Turns to* DRAKE.) it as a most unlooked-for blessing if you, too, have been struck by sanity.

DRAKE. (*Slight pause.*) You will not get out of here, Millington. Oh, in a year or two. Five, perhaps. Or even (*Rises and crosses to him.*) ten. Until then we are to be graced with your presence.

MILLINGTON. (*Turns to him.*) . . . What are you talking about?

DRAKE. I am quoting the Adjutant—"My dear fellow." They intend to keep you here, Millington. They have duties for you. Of an unpleasant kind.

MILLINGTON. (*Jumps up.*) I don't believe you!

DRAKE. (*Bitterly.*) Why don't you ask him?! (*Crosses D. of* MILLINGTON *to* D. L. *table.* DRAKE'S *bitterness convinces* MILLINGTON. *He sits again slowly.*) The option lies with them.

MILLINGTON. (*Turns to him.*) . . . But why? Why?!

DRAKE. (*Turns to him.*) You are to be taught a lesson, Millington. You are to learn that this Regiment is not mocked.

MILLINGTON. . . . My God. I never thought of that.

DRAKE. (*Bitterly.*) No more did I.

(HUTTON *comes on.*)

HUTTON. Stand up!

(MILLINGTON *now much shaken. The Court files on as before. It is clear at once that* SENIOR SUBALTERN *and* ADJUTANT *are angry with* DRAKE. *From their positions they glare at him.*)

ADJUTANT. Be seated, gentlemen. (*All sit.* HUTTON *closes doors and sits.*) This Court is now in session.

MILLINGTON. (*Rises.*) Mister President, I must tell you . . .

ADJUTANT. Be silent, Mister Millington!

MILLINGTON. But . . .

ADJUTANT. If you speak again, I shall have you put out at once. Now sit down, sir. (MILLINGTON *sits. It has been an automatic gesture of protest. What could he say?*) Mister Fothergill.

SENIOR SUBALTERN. (*Rises, crosses below witness chair to below* R. *end court table.*) Mister President. As you already know—and as I now inform the Court—Mister Drake has this afternoon insisted that Mrs. Hasseltine appear before this Court. He will not accept a written deposition from her. (HART *and others are astonished.*)

ADJUTANT. (*Furious. Glares at* DRAKE.) I am indeed aware of that, Mister Fothergill.

SENIOR SUBALTERN. (*All look at* FOTHERGILL.) I therefore propose to call her now, Mister President. (*Crosses* R. *above witness chair to his chair.*)

ADJUTANT. Mr. Hutton.

HUTTON. Sir. (*Exits, opening both doors.*)

DRAKE. (*Alarmed, rises.*) But— (*This planned move is a shock to* DRAKE.)

ADJUTANT. You have wanted to question Mrs. Hasseltine, Mister Drake. Very well. Now you shall.

DRAKE. (*Worried.*) I had no wish to call her yet, Mr. President.

ADJUTANT. That is your misfortune, Mr. Drake. This Court has not been convened to satisfy your wishes.

HUTTON. (*Enters to his chair.*) Would you come this way, please, ma'am . . .

ADJUTANT. You will rise, gentlemen. (*All rise.*)

MRS. HASSELTINE. (*Entering.*) Thank you, Mr. Hutton. (*She crosses to* D. R. *of* TRULY, *apparently gracious and calm.*)

ADJUTANT. (*Bows.*) Ma'am. (*All click and bow.*)

MRS. HASSELTINE. Mister President.

ADJUTANT. I am sorry that you should have been disturbed in this way, ma'am. I trust you will appreciate it is not of our choosing.

MRS. HASSELTINE. (*Bravely understanding.*) I understand that *very* well, Mister President. I have, besides, no objection to appearing before this enquiry.

ADJUTANT. Thank you, ma'am. (*All bow.*) Please be seated. (*Indicates witness chair.*)

MRS. HASSELTINE. Thank you. . . . (*In moving to witness chair, she faces* DRAKE. *A moment of antipathy.* TRULY *goes behind witness chair, bows and returns to seat. When* MRS. HASSELTINE *sits, all sit.*)

ADJUTANT. (*Breathlessly.*) Mister Fothergill . . .

SENIOR SUBALTERN. (*Comes down: bows deeply, crosses to her* R.) Ma'am . . .

MRS. HASSELTINE. Mister Fothergill . . .

SENIOR SUBALTERN. I should like to ask you just three

questions, ma'am. Were you attacked on the seventeenth of this month?

MRS. HASSELTINE. I was, yes.

SENIOR SUBALTERN. By whom, ma'am?

MRS. HASSELTINE. By Mister Millington.

SENIOR SUBALTERN. There is no doubt in your mind as to that?

MRS. HASSELTINE. None whatever. Mister Millington made both his identity and his intentions absolutely plain to me.

SENIOR SUBALTERN. Thank you, ma'am. (*Bows deeply. Returns to his place, sits.*)

ADJUTANT. Mister Drake.

(DRAKE *rises, bows to President. Recovered from surprise, he proceeds to outmanoeuvre them. He is learning guile—and discovering toughness, stubbornness in himself.*)

DRAKE. Mister President. I am most anxious to conduct myself in accordance with the requirements laid down by you for this Court. However, it would greatly assist me in . . . presenting a coherent account to this Court . . . if you would permit me to call another witness before I question Mrs. Hasseltine. (*Reaction.* HART *looks at* ADJUTANT.)

ADJUTANT. Certainly not, Mister Drake. Mrs. Hasseltine has already been greatly inconvenienced, entirely on your account. You will ask your questions now.

DRAKE. . . . With respect, Mister President, I am most anxious not to inconvenience Mrs. Hasseltine further. (*Bows to her.*) But since I am not yet presenting the case for the Defence, I should merely be obliged to recall her at a later date. (FOTHERGILL *and* HART *impatiently look to* ADJUTANT.) Whereas this other matter would take but a moment or two—I do assure you, ma'am; and you, Mister— (*All look at* DRAKE.)

ADJUTANT. You will not be allowed to recall Mrs. Hasseltine later, Mister Drake!

ACT II CONDUCT UNBECOMING 79

DRAKE. . . . Again with respect, Mister President, it is my entitlement—as laid down by you before all the members of this Court—to call any witness of whatever rank or station, should I require to do so. (*Apprehensive looks to* ADJUTANT.)

(*A pause.* HARPER *is trapped.*)

ADJUTANT. . . . Whom do you wish to call?
DRAKE. The Second in Command, Mister President. (*A shock to all.*)
ADJUTANT. . . . Major Roach?
DRAKE. Yes, Mister President.
ADJUTANT. . . . Is he aware of this?
DRAKE. He is waiting in the Card Room, sir.
ADJUTANT. (*Looks* L. *to Card Room.*) Very well. (*Rises. He is outranked.*) I am sorry, ma'am. It appears that Mister Drake is determined to put you to the greatest possible inconvenience. I wonder if I might ask you . . . ?
MRS. HASSELTINE. (*Rises. All rise.*) Yes, of course, Mister President. I am only too anxious to assist you in this enquiry.
ADJUTANT. Ma'am . . . (*All bow.*)
MRS. HASSELTINE. (HUTTON *opens doors.*) Gentlemen. . . . (*Looks at* DRAKE. *Clearly disturbed, she goes* R. *doors.* HARPER *is furious. All swivel look at* DRAKE *and sit.* ADJUTANT *remains standing.*)
ADJUTANT. I am not pleased by this, Mister Drake.
DRAKE. . . . I am sorry, Mister President.
ADJUTANT. Mr. Boulton. (BOULTON *rises.*) Call the Second in Command. (BOULTON ["*Sir!*"] *goes off* [*a different way*], L. *arch. Silence. Stiffness.* MILLINGTON *murmurs to* DRAKE.)
MILLINGTON. But why? why him . . . ? (DRAKE *shushes* MILLINGTON.)
ADJUTANT. I've no doubt that if you can contain yourself in patience, Mr. Millington, Mr. Drake will enlighten us all.

(*They sit:* HARPER *remains standing.* BOULTON *returns with* SECOND IN COMMAND [*frosty disapproval*] D. L. *arch. Crosses* R. *to witness chair.*)

BOULTON. (*At his place.*) Sir . . .
ADJUTANT. (*Bows.*) Sir.
ROACH. Mister Harper.
ADJUTANT. Be seated, sir, please.
ROACH. . . . Thank you. (*Sits: his disapproval of the Court is quite apparent.* BOULTON *sits.*)
ADJUTANT. (*Sits.*) Mister Drake . . .
DRAKE. (*Rises.*) Sir. Is it a fact that when you sent for me as defending officer, this morning, you told me that you had witnessed the attack on Mrs. Hasseltine by Mister Millington? (*Reaction.* FOTHERGILL *turns fast.* HART *leans forward.*)
ROACH. I did, yes. (*Shock to Court.*)
DRAKE. In what circumstances, sir?
ROACH. I was Officer of the Week. Mister Hart was Officer of the Day. At about two o'clock we were just completing our final tour of inspection. I had sent Mister Hart down to look over the native lines while I myself was crossing via the Folly to inspect the perimeter piquet on the Plain.
DRAKE. Yes, sir.
ROACH. As I was passing the Folly, I heard what sounded like some sort of altercation among the shrubbery and trees surrounding. I stopped. And then I heard Mister Millington's voice. I am not certain as to what he said, except that he appeared to be pleading with someone. But then I heard Mrs. Hasseltine—very sharply and clearly. She said: "I have already told you, Mister Millington, that I find your advances not only . . . offensive to me, but quite pointless." Or words very much to that effect. (FOTHERGILL *is taking notes.*)
DRAKE. She must have sounded angry, sir.
ROACH. She did, indeed. Extremely.
DRAKE. And frightened?

ROACH. No. I would have said she sounded—in command of the situation, rather than afraid.

DRAKE. . . . I see. And then, sir? (*All react, puzzled.*)

ROACH. Well, I immediately stepped in among the trees to put an end to this nonsense. But it was extremely dark in there, Mister Drake—in the end I could make them out only from their voices—and then against the paler colour of the stonework.

DRAKE. They were fighting, sir?

ROACH. Mister Millington had hold of Mrs. Hasseltine's (FOTHERGILL *makes note.*) arm. But before I could intervene, she had broken away from him—had ordered him to leave her alone—and had begun to walk angrily back through the trees towards the Mess.

DRAKE. (*Crosses* R. *to him, fast.*) To walk, sir?

ROACH. Yes.

DRAKE. Not to run?

ROACH. No, no. I could see her quite clearly. The lights of the Mess were directly beyond her, if you understand me. About thirty or forty yards away.

DRAKE. Still, she must have appeared extremely distressed.

ROACH. I should have said . . . angry, rather than distressed.

DRAKE. (*Looks at* ADJUTANT. *Crosses* L. *to* MILLINGTON.) I see. What happened then, sir?

ROACH. Well, you know what happened next, Mister Drake. There was great consternation. The other gentleman running, myself included. And when I got into the Mess, rather to my surprise, Mrs. Hasseltine was indeed in an anguished condition. Extremely so. Far more than I should have imagined.

DRAKE. Why do you say that, sir?

ROACH. Well . . . there is no excuse for Mister Millington's behaviour. None whatever. It was in every sense reprehensible. However, it had not appeared to me quite so—shocking. Quite so—violent or extreme.

DRAKE. Would it be fair to say, sir, that it was your

impression that this was a . . . feeble and unsuccessful attempt on the part of a younger man to force his attentions on an older woman?

ROACH. . . . That would have been my impression, yes. But . . .

ADJUTANT. I must intervene, sir. Exactly what are you trying to establish by this testimony, Mr. Drake?

DRAKE. I am merely anxious that the Court should have the . . . clearest possible understanding of what occurred, Mr. President.

ADJUTANT. (FOTHERGILL *uncomfortable*.) . . . I see. But has not the Second in Command just given an extremely detailed account of precisely the offence with which Mister Milington is charged? (*Slightly rises. To* SECOND IN COMMAND.) Is that not so, sir?

ROACH. I have, yes. And he should be disciplined for it. (*Angrily*.) But certainly not by an affair of this kind. (FOTHERGILL *and Court tense*.) You know my views in this matter, Mister Harper. (*An intense whisper*.) The Regiment is ill-served by manifestations of this nature.

ADJUTANT. . . . But would it not be greatly less well served by the alternative, sir?

ROACH. That may be the case. At least it would have the sanction of proper authority behind it.

ADJUTANT. . . . Yes, sir.

ROACH. (*Glares.* FOTHERGILL *cringes*.) Very well. I shall express myself—forcibly, gentlemen—at a later stage.

ADJUTANT. Sir. Mister Drake.

DRAKE. Finally, sir, I should like to ask what became of Mister Millington in all of this?

ROACH. I understand, from what you have told me, that he was knocked down by Mrs. Hasseltine. Which is perfectly possible. My view was not clear. Certainly she broke from him with some force. For my own part, I had thought that he had made off into the trees. I had intended to deal with the matter myself, you see. To speak to Mrs. Hasseltine as soon as I returned to the Mess.

DRAKE. But you were overtaken by events?
ROACH. Unhappily, yes, I was.
DRAKE. Thank you, sir. (*Bows. He sits, takes notes.*)
ADJUTANT. . . . I wish to be clear as to exactly what you are saying, sir. You are telling this Court that you witnessed Mister Millington's attack on Mrs. Hasseltine?
ROACH. In essence, yes. Though, as I say, it was dark.
ADJUTANT. There is no doubt in your mind as to the identity (*Points at* MILLINGTON.) of Mister Millington?
ROACH. None whatever.
ADJUTANT. I see. (*Rises.*) Then I don't think we need to detain you any further, sir. . . . (*Looks to* SENIOR SUBALTERN *who shakes head.*) Thank you for coming to give evidence before us, sir.
ROACH. (*Rises, angry look at them.*) Gentlemen . . . (*Goes,* D. L. *arch.*)
ADJUTANT. (*Sits.*) Perhaps I should remind you, Mister Drake, that you are here to defend this officer, not to prosecute him. (FOTHERGILL *leads laughter. General amusement.*)
DRAKE. (*Rises.*) Thank you, Mister President. In the circumstances of this trial, it is as well to be reminded of why we are here. (*All react.* FOTHERGILL *slaps papers down.*)
ADJUTANT. . . . Do you still wish to question Mrs. Hasseltine?
DRAKE. (*Rises.*) Yes, Mister President, I do.
ADJUTANT. Very well. Mr. Hutton.
HUTTON. Sir. (*Goes off,* R. *doors.*)
ADJUTANT. I will remind you, Mister Drake, to be courteous. (*Stands.*)
HUTTON. Will you come in now, please, ma'am. (*Shows on* MRS. HASSELTINE, *who is clearly annoyed, cool.* [*And who is wondering.*])
ADJUTANT. You will rise, gentlemen.
HUTTON. Ma'am.
ADJUTANT. Ma'am. (*All bow.*) I do not think we shall need to detain you for more than a moment or two longer.

Mrs. Hasseltine. Very well.

Adjutant. Please . . . (*Gestures to chair.*)

Mrs. Hasseltine. Thank you. . . . (Truly *repeats chair bit. She sits. They all sit.* Hutton *closes doors. The antipathy between her and* Drake *is palpable, yet unstated.* Drake *has remained standing.*)

Drake. (*Moves* r., *fast.* Adjutant *stops him.*) Mrs. Hasseltine . . .

Adjutant. Before Mr. Drake begins to question you, (Drake *crosses* d. l. c.) ma'am, I should perhaps tell you that the Second in Command has just informed this Court that he witnessed Mr. Millington's attack (Drake *turns to* Adjutant.) on you.

Mrs. Hasseltine. . . . I see. Thank you, Mister President.

Adjutant. Ma'am. Mister Drake . . .

Drake. Mrs. Hasseltine. The Second in Command has indeed made it perfectly plain that Mister Millington's behaviour was totally improper.

Mrs. Hasseltine. It was indeed.

Drake. It must have been . . . very frightening for you, ma'am.

Mrs. Hasseltine. It is hardly agreeable to be attacked in the darkness, Mister Drake.

Adjutant. Just so, Mister Drake.

Drake. Particularly in so isolated a spot.

Mrs. Hasseltine. As you say.

Drake. (*Crosses* d. l. *of* c., *turns front.*) I am . . . wondering how you came to be there, ma'am?

Mrs. Hasseltine. (*Smiles.*) There is no mystery as to *that*, Mister Drake. There is a stone bench there. You may not have been with us long enough *yet* to have discovered it.

Drake. (*Smiles to her.*) I discovered it this afternoon, ma'am. Indeed I, ah, sampled it. You cannot have found it more comfortable . . . perhaps more convenient than a seat here, in the Mess?

MRS. HASSELTINE. (*Smiles.*) Were you a woman, Mister Drake, you would understand that—even at the most enjoyable ball, where one is outnumbered—there *are* moments when one wishes to be alone.

DRAKE. (*Crosses* R. *to* C.) Just so, ma'am. (*Bows.*) And it was here, at the bench, that Mister Millington . . . disturbed you?

MRS. HASSELTINE. He did, yes.

DRAKE. (*Springs close.*) He . . . sprang out at you? (*Court not amused.*)

MRS. HASSELTINE. Well—hardly that, Mister Drake.

DRAKE. He spoke to you?

MRS. HASSELTINE. . . . Yes.

DRAKE. In, forgive me, in an improper manner?

MRS. HASSELTINE. . . . *Yes.*

DRAKE. And you . . . rose at once to leave? You called out?

MRS. HASSELTINE. Not at once, no.

DRAKE. You did not think it necessary, ma'am?

MRS. HASSELTINE. I did not at once realize how drunk nor how determined he was.

DRAKE. I see. You did not want to get him into trouble?

MRS. HASSELTINE. *No.* Not then. I thought he was just being stupid.

DRAKE. But he persisted.

MRS. HASSELTINE. He did indeed. He made it quite plain why he was doing so. (*To* FOTHERGILL.)

DRAKE. Well, forgive me, ma'am . . . (*Crosses* R. *of her, above witness chair.*) But you are an extremely attractive woman. You must have found yourself having to deal with silly young gentlemen before this? (*Shock—Court.*)

ADJUTANT. Mr. Drake, it is of no concern to this Court what may have happened in the past.

DRAKE. . . . It was intended purely as a general observation, Mister President.

MRS. HASSELTINE. I am *not* accustomed to having to

deal with young men who are—determinedly and viciously drunk, Mister Drake.

DRAKE. (R. *of her.*) . . . Viciously drunk, ma'am?

MRS. HASSELTINE. Mister Millington made it absolutely plain that he was determined to use me as a means of having himself dismissed from this Regiment. (*Shock— Court. Eyes on* MILLINGTON. HART *and* BOULTON *take notes.*)

DRAKE. I see. And so you were compelled to fight him?

MRS. HASSELTINE. . . . I *was,* yes.

DRAKE. To hit him?

MRS. HASSELTINE. *Yes.*

DRAKE. With what, ma'am? (*All turn to* MRS. HASSELTINE.)

MRS. HASSELTINE. *Well!* . . . My fists . . . my arms. Whatever came to hand.

DRAKE. And did anything come to hand, ma'am? (HART *and* BOULTON *lean forward, looking towards* MRS. HASSELTINE.)

MRS. HASSELTINE. . . . I don't understand you, Mister Drake.

DRAKE. You struck him with your fan perhaps?

MRS. HASSELTINE. I must have done, yes.

DRAKE. Or your bag?

MRS. HASSELTINE. I imagine so.

DRAKE. Were you carrying anything else?

MRS. HASSELTINE. No—why?

DRAKE. Did you perhaps pick up a stone?

MRS. HASSELTINE. (*Turns* U.) . . . I don't think so, no.

DRAKE. (*Crosses* U., *stopped by* ADJUTANT.) Or a fallen branch?

ADJUTANT. I think, ma'am, that Mister Drake is referring—

DRAKE. (*Fast cross* D. *to* L. *of witness chair.*) I am referring to the injury sustained by Mister Millington, ma'am. There is a gash—an extremely unpleasant gash, about two inches long—behind his ear.

Mrs. Hasseltine. Well, that's right—yes. I do remember now—that I struck at him. With my arm. Like that. (*Demonstrates downward blow.*)

Drake. (Fothergill *is annoyed.*) With your right arm?

Mrs. Hasseltine. Yes. Well . . . yes, I think so . . .

Drake. Are you right-handed, Mrs. Hasseltine?

Mrs. Hasseltine. . . . Yes, I am.

Drake. (*Drily: convinced now she lies.*) Were you standing behind him at the time, ma'am?

Mrs. Hasseltine. . . . I'm afraid I don't . . .

Drake. (*Fast cross to* d. l. *table.*) The injury is to the right-hand side of his head, Mrs. Hasseltine.

Mrs. Hasseltine. . . . Well, really, Mister Drake! We were fighting! In the darkness! I really cannot be expected—

Adjutant. Exactly so, Mister Drake. You are asking the witness to remember events that happened at a time of great stress for her. (*Turns to her.*)

Mrs. Hasseltine. Just so, Mister President . . .

Drake. (*Quickly. Turns to her.*) I am sorry, ma'am. Forgive me. It is quite unreasonable of me to expect you to remember details of that kind.

Adjutant. . . . Very well, Mister Drake.

Drake. We may take it, however, that you did hit him? (Fothergill *sighs.*)

Adjutant. We have already taken that, Mister Drake.

Mrs. Hasseltine. . . . I *did*, yes.

Drake. (*Very clearly.*) With what, ma'am?

Mrs. Hasseltine. Perhaps it was a stone, as you say. . . .

Drake. (*Fast cross* l. *of* Mrs. Hasseltine.) I do not think so, ma'am. . . .

Adjutant. Mr. Drake . . .

Drake. I searched the Folly for all of three hours this afternoon, ma'am. I found no vestige of one for over a hundred yards in any direction.

Mrs. Hasseltine. Then it must have been a branch—

DRAKE. There is nothing, Mrs. Hasseltine. Not a stick. Not a stone. Nothing with which you could possibly have struck Mister Millington. (MILLINGTON *looks up.*) Nothing that could be lifted by a dozen men, let alone by one woman!

MRS. HASSELTINE. Really, this is too absurd!	ADJUTANT. Really, Mr. Drake. (DRAKE *turns to* ADJUTANT.) It is surely not beyond your powers of imagination, Mister Drake, to realise that Mister Millington probably fell back against a tree, or against the wall, when Mrs. Hasseltine broke away from him.

MRS. HASSELTINE. Exactly so, Mister President. . . .

MILLINGTON. I was hit, Mr. President . . .

ADJUTANT. Be silent, sir!

(*Together.* ADJUTANT *and* DRAKE *turn on* MILLINGTON.)	MILLINGTON. She hit me! (*Jumps up—points.*)
	DRAKE. Be quiet!
	ADJUTANT. Will you be quiet, sir!

MRS. HASSELTINE. (*Strained.*) Of course, if you prefer to accept the word of the accused officer as against that of myself . . .

ADJUTANT. (MILLINGTON *sits.*) Certainly not, ma'am. That does not arise. Mister Drake, this has gone far enough.

DRAKE. (*Hurriedly.*) I am sorry, Mister President . . .

ADJUTANT. You will end your questions now.

DRAKE. But I only have a question or two more, Mister President (ADJUTANT—*gesture of resignation to* HART.) —and I readily accept that this was a misunderstanding on my part. (*Turns to her.*) I see now that Mister Millington probably fell back against this wall, or tree, ma'am, and that you escaped from him. And that you then ran—screaming—a matter of forty yards or so to the Mess. (*Crosses* U. L. *of her.*)

ADJUTANT. Mister Drake. We already have the evidence of the Second in Command that in the first instance—

DRAKE. (*Turns to him.*) Of course, Mister President. I am sorry. (*To* MRS. HASSELTINE.) In the first instance you walked, ma'am. (*Slight pause. Crosses to* R. *of witness chair* [*above it*].) And then perhaps you ran? Perhaps you feared he might attack you again?

MRS. HASSELTINE. . . . That thought did enter my mind, yes.

DRAKE. He didn't, of course, ma'am?

MRS. HASSELTINE. No, Mister Drake, he did not.

DRAKE. Then he must have attacked you with extreme severity on the first occasion. Exactly what did he do, ma'am?

MRS. HASSELTINE. Well, he . . .

DRAKE. Did he take hold of your arm?

MRS. HASSELTINE. He did, yes.

DRAKE. And he pulled you about?

MRS. HASSELTINE. Yes.

DRAKE. And then, ma'am?

MRS. HASSELTINE. Well, he . . .

DRAKE. Yes, ma'am?

MRS. HASSELTINE. . . . Really, I cannot be expected to remember—

DRAKE. Well, did he perhaps attempt to place his hand on your bosom? (*All are shocked.*) Your dress was torn— (*She looks to* ADJUTANT.)

ADJUTANT. Mister Drake—

MRS. HASSELTINE. He *may* have done, yes.

DRAKE. (*Crosses above* L. *of her.*) Well, did he, or didn't he, ma'am?

MRS. HASSELTINE. I can't remember, Mister Drake!

DRAKE. But this was a terrifying experience for you, Mrs. Hasseltine. You ran, screaming, all the way into the Mess!

MRS. HASSELTINE. (*Rises: blazing.*) Exactly what are you implying?!

ADJUTANT. (*Jumps up.*) That is all, Mister Drake! Sit down!

DRAKE. (*Turns* U. *to* ADJUTANT *across court table.*) I have only one more question for this—

ADJUTANT. (*Points* L. DRAKE *loses battle and slowly crosses* L. *to* D. L. *table.*) No, Mister Drake! Be seated!

(*Pause.*)

DRAKE. (*Fast turn.*) Why are you lying, Mrs. Hasseltine? (*Court is shocked.* FOTHERGILL *through ceiling.*)

ADJUTANT. Mister Drake!

MRS. HASSELTINE. (*Jumps up.*) How dare you! How dare you, Mister Drake!

ADJUTANT. Ma'am, I am sorry. This—

MRS. HASSELTINE. Mr. President, (*Storming out: crossing up* R. *steps—stops, turns.* HUTTON *opens doors.*) I shall tolerate no more of this! You may play your childish games in future without me! (*She is gone. A shocked silence.* MILLINGTON *dazed, baffled. In silence the* ADJUTANT *comes round the table and down to* DRAKE. HUTTON *closes doors. All look at* DRAKE.)

ADJUTANT. (*Kicks chair back, comes round* R. *of table and* L. *to* DRAKE.) You have finished yourself here, Mister Drake. Do you hear me? You are finished here.

DRAKE. (*Sick at heart.*) . . . If what I have heard in this courtroom . . . is typical of the honour of this Regiment . . . then I shall be only too happy to depart.

ADJUTANT. And we shall be only too happy to accommodate you. (*Turns away* D. C., *faces front.*) Now the rest of you, pay attention to me.

DRAKE. That woman is lying, Mister Harper. (FOTHERGILL *can't believe ears.*)

ADJUTANT. Be silent, sir! (*Pause.*) This Court will reconvene at midnight tomorrow, when this matter will be ended. You hear me, Mister Drake? Ended!

DRAKE. (*Pause: nods slowly.*) . . . Yes, Mister President.

ADJUTANT. Very well. That is all. (*All rise.* HUTTON *opens doors.* ADJUTANT *stalks out,* R. *doors. Pause. The others leave . . . as before.* HUTTON *closes* U. *door.* FOTHERGILL *closes* D. *door.* DRAKE, MILLINGTON *alone.* DRAKE *is near to tears, but for him this is not possible.* MILLINGTON *has no way to express sympathy for this man. Pause.*)

DRAKE. (*Sits.*) . . . I thought this was a Regiment of honour.

MILLINGTON. (*Crosses* U. *of* DRAKE. *Embarrassed.*) So it is, my dear fellow. A Regiment of the highest honour. As you yourself have made plain to me.

DRAKE. . . . It appears that I owe you an apology, Mister Millington. (*A pause.*)

MILLINGTON. What's going on, Arthur?

DRAKE. I do not know.

MILLINGTON. (*Crosses to below* C. *of court table.*) Why should she lie?

DRAKE. . . . It may be that she isn't.

MILLINGTON. But she fetched me the devil of a crack.

DRAKE. . . . Why don't you go to bed?

MILLINGTON. Why not? (*Starts to go, stops, leans* L. *end court table. In his own way, flippant, awkward, tries to help.*) You know, Arthur, if you . . . wish to remain here . . . you really will have to abandon this enterprise. It isn't too late.

DRAKE. . . . I can survive without your sympathy, Millington. Yours least of all.

MILLINGTON. You disappoint me, Arthur. Is it just pride, then? Wounded pride?

DRAKE. . . . Let us call it principle. Why not? "Bourgeois" principle. But that, of course, is something you would not understand. (*Turns away.*)

MILLINGTON. No. That is true. I am told, though, that it is invincible.

DRAKE. Are you? Well. (*Turns: great pain.*) Then you have met . . . an invincible man, have you not?

MILLINGTON. (*Crosses* L., *touches* DRAKE'S *shoulder.*) . . . Good night, Arthur. (*Goes quickly,* L. *arch. Pause. At last* DRAKE *covers his face in pain. A grunt comes from him.*)

DRAKE. Oh, God . . . ! (*Leans forward, head in hands.*)

(PRADAH SINGH *comes urgently on,* U. R. *arch.*)

PRADAH. Sahib . . . ! Sahib! (*Crosses* D. *to below* C. *of court table.*)

DRAKE. . . . Yes?

PRADAH. (*Crosses to* D. L. *corner court table.*) Mrs. Bandanai is here, sahib . . . !

DRAKE. (*Absorbed: almost indifferent.*) Ah . . . Yes. Thank you, Pradah Singh. . . .

PRADAH. She was attacked, too, sahib.

DRAKE. (*Becoming alert. Rises.*) Attacked?

PRADAH. Yes, sahib.

DRAKE. When?

PRADAH. I do not know, sahib, but—

DRAKE. Where is she?

PRADAH. . . . She is outside. (*Starts* R.)

DRAKE. (*Briskly: turning away.*) Bring her in.

PRADAH. (*Stops* R. *side court table.*) In here, sahib? It is not proper.

DRAKE. (*Crosses to* R. *end court table.*) Bring her in, Pradah Singh! That's an order.

PRADAH. . . . Sahib. (*Unwilling,* PRADAH SINGH *goes* U. R. DRAKE *paces, impatient.* PRADAH SINGH *returns, steering* MRS. BANDANAI *by grip on elbow.* "*Ya ha-ya ha.*" *She enters, crosses* D. R. *of court table, above witness chair.* PRADAH *straightens* ADJUTANT'S *chair, crosses* R. *to steps, above* MRS. BANDANAI. DRAKE D. L. C. MRS. BANDANAI *is withdrawn, unwilling, hides face.* PRADAH SINGH *disapproves of, resists what follows.*) This is Mrs. Bandanai, sahib.

DRAKE. Sit down, ma'am, please.
PRADAH. Bato. Bato. (*She sits witness chair.* PRADAH *crosses to* L. *of witness chair.*)
DRAKE. Doesn't she speak English?
PRADAH. No, sahib. (*Pause.*) She does not wish to speak at all, sahib.
DRAKE. Tell her I mean her no harm.
PRADAH. Tumhea musselat may nakin delavgay.
DRAKE. Tell her . . . there is a young officer in trouble.
PRADAH. Ik offcer takf lif may mi hay.
DRAKE. I wish to help him.
PRADAH. Uski sahab madat karna chahaté hé.
DRAKE. But without her I cannot.
PRADAH. Opké sewa sevay madat nehi hosakti.
MRS. BANDANAI. Engarasi suar ko main kum madat marun, una merna do, muja keya parya.
PRADAH. Bas! Bas!
DRAKE. What did she say?
PRADAH. . . . She is overwrought, sahib. (*To* MRS. BANDANAI.) A sāmat bolo.
DRAKE. No. Tell me what she said.
PRADAH. Very well. She said, "Why should I help the English swine? Let him die, I don't care."

(*Pause.* DRAKE *suddenly crisp, anger and obsession growing.*)

DRAKE. Ask her if it is true that she was attacked.
PRADAH. Keya kaya such hai apko kesiné hat lagaya?
MRS. BANDANAI. Je hain such hai.
PRADAH. It is true, sahib.
DRAKE. When?
PRADAH. . . . Sahib, I cannot . . .
DRAKE. Ask her when.
PRADAH. Kab? Kab?
MRS. BANDANAI. Cha mana pahla.
PRADAH. Jut! Chut jut!
MRS. BANDANAI. Nahin, nahin, main jut nahin bolte!

DRAKE. What does she say, Pradah Singh?!

PRADAH. She says . . . six months ago, sahib.

DRAKE. Six months ago! Ask her who, Pradah Singh.

PRADAH. Sahib, I . . .

DRAKE. Ask her who! (DRAKE *obsessively demanding now: if understandable, also unpleasant.*)

PRADAH. (*Breaks* R. *above witness chair.*) Kuan tha?

MRS. BANDANAI. Nahin bataguin! Nahin bataguin!

PRADAH. (*Turns to him.*) She will not tell you, sahib.

DRAKE. Ask her what happened, then.

PRADAH. Sahib, I am not in a position . . .

DRAKE. (*Crosses to her.*) Ask her!

PRADAH. (*Kneels* R. *of her.*) Keya hua?

MRS. BANDANAI. Main ek offcer ke sath thee, uska sath suithee, ekali thee, wa bungla chor ka chalagaya.

PRADAH. . . . She was with an officer. She had been with him, lain with him, sahib. . . . She was alone though, he had left the bungalow.

MRS. BANDANAI. Nagi thee, char payee ke upar.

PRADAH. She was naked, sahib, naked on the bed.

MRS. BANDANAI. Ethna mai ek admi aya, gera lal aur suana ke tera.

PRADAH. There came another man, I think she said, another man in scarlet and gold. (DRAKE *kneels* L. *of witness chair.*)

MRS. BANDANAI. Unena maja kaha char payee sa utho, hath aur paun sa duro.

PRADAH. He made her get off the bed, sahib, he made her crawl about on her hands and knees. . . .

MRS. BANDANAI. Aur suar ke tera awaz be bano. Eska pas telwar be thee.

PRADAH. She had to make noises, noises like a . . . (*Rises, turns. Crosses to above* D. R. *table.*) he had a sword . . .

DRAKE. You don't . . . ?

PRADAH. . . . It is the game, it is the game, sahib, as they play it in the Mess. Sticking the pig. With a sword. From behind. As it runs . . .

DRAKE. Oh, my God. . . . No. . . . (*Breaks* L. *below court table.*)

PRADAH. (*Crosses to her, kneels* R. *of her.*) It is the game, I am certain. . . . (DRAKE *shocked, sickened, almost as if he might sink into a chair.* PRADAH *soothes* MRS. BANDANAI.) Teekeh hai theke hai.

MRS. BANDANAI. Bahutu buri bath hui, bahutu buri bath hui.

DRAKE. (*Turns to* PRADAH.) . . . But who . . . Who could do such a thing?

PRADAH. Nam bolo, nam bolo?

MRS. BANDANAI. Engaras . . .

PRADAH. An Englishman, sahib.

DRAKE. (*Crosses to her.*) Who? Ask her who, Pradah Singh! Tell her I must know! Tell her I will find this man! That I will stop him! That I will not cover up the truth!

PRADAH. Nam bata-o.

MRS. BANDANAI. Main nahin bata sakti, muja janhan sa pension melta hai, mai kesi par dosh nahin laga sakti.

PRADAH. She cannot tell you, sahib, she has a pension from this Regiment. How can she accuse . . .

DRAKE. A pension! For God's sake! This is my life! This is my life! (*Crosses below* L. *of her. Takes her hands.*)

MRS. BANDANAI. (*Rises, breaks away from him.*) Scarlett. Captain Scarlett! (*Crosses* U. R. *of court table to veranda* C.)

PRADAH. Chut! Chut! (*Follows,* DRAKE *fast cross to* U. S. L.)

MRS. BANDANAI. Main such bolti huin. Main such bolti huin. Captain Scarlett! (*Exits* U. L.)

PRADAH. (*On veranda* C.) Wapas auo wapas auo.

(*She runs out of the room. Silence.*)

DRAKE. Captain Scarlett . . . ?

PRADAH. (*Turns front,* C. *of veranda.*) Yes, sahib.

DRAKE. (*Crosses R. to showcase.*) . . . But . . .
PRADAH. He was killed in the Mutiny, sahib.
DRAKE. He's dead! (*Crosses D. to above witness chair.*)
PRADAH. Yes, sahib. Captain Scarlett—is dead.
DRAKE. What's happening . . . ?

CURTAIN

ACT THREE

Scene 1

The Mess. The trial. The next midnight. MILLINGTON *is waiting,* U. R. C. *pillar, clearly worried.* DRAKE *comes on,* R. *doors, carrying a paper-wrapped package which he places on the defence table. He fast crosses* D. L. *with bundle, puts parcel on* D. L. *table. Each in his own way is embarrassed and awkward.*

MILLINGTON. (*Crosses* D. C.) Arthur, I must . . . speak with you—
DRAKE. (*Crosses* R. *below court table to meet him.*) And I, you—
MILLINGTON. I have been thinking, my dear fellow, and, ah—
DRAKE. I know now that you spoke the truth, Millington.
MILLINGTON. . . . What?
DRAKE. You may have been stupid, but you were not vicious.
MILLINGTON. No . . . Besides, I rather like her, as a matter of fact. . . .
DRAKE. . . . Look here. I want you to trust me, Millington. Tonight's proceedings will not be pleasant, but you must remain silent whatever happens.
MILLINGTON. (*Awkwardly.*) That is what I wanted to speak to you about. . . .
DRAKE. . . . What?
MILLINGTON. Arthur—I— (*Awkward. Crosses* D. L. *to* D. L. *table.*) Look here, Arthur, I went riding this morning . . .
DRAKE. (*Turns to him.*) I'm afraid I don't—
MILLINGTON. No, no, let me finish, please. . . . I re-

ceived this note from the Colonel. Yes. (*Leans* D. *end* D. L. *table.*) "The Colonel presents his compliments to Mr. Millington, and wonders whether Mr. Millington might care to exercise the Colonel's string again. The Colonel would of course be grateful if Mr. Millington would endeavour to maintain contact with the Colonel's animals on this occasion." I like horses, Arthur. . . . (*Pause.*)

DRAKE. Millington . . .

MILLINGTON. It is in one, do you see, Arthur? One is not to escape. I felt this morning, as you must . . . that one is . . . intended for a particular place. (DRAKE *looks away, breaks* R. *to* R. *of* C.) So you see, Arthur, you are . . . (*Crosses* R. *to him.*) destroying yourself here for no reason. . . . I . . .

DRAKE. You are not to concern yourself with me.

MILLINGTON. But I do, Arthur, I do. . . . I know what this place means to you.

DRAKE. No. (*Turns to him.*) No. I do not expect to remain here. . . . (HUTTON *comes on.*)

HUTTON. Come to order!

(*The Court files on as before, the* ADJUTANT *last to his place. He looks furiously at* DRAKE. DRAKE *and* MILLINGTON *to their places.*)

ADJUTANT. (*Crosses* L. *to* DRAKE.) Before I convene this court, I am told, Mister Drake, that you have recalled the Doctor.

DRAKE. Yes, Mister President, I have.

ADJUTANT. I told you this matter would be ended tonight, and it will be!

DRAKE. So it will, Mister President—that I guarantee.

ADJUTANT. (*Crosses* U. R. *of table to his chair. Pause.*) Very well. Be seated, gentlemen. (*They all do so.*) This court is now in session. Mister Fothergill?

SENIOR SUBALTERN. (*Rises, crosses to* D. R. *end court table.*) I have no more witnesses to call, Mister President. I have here written depositions from the Colonel, Major

ACT III   CONDUCT UNBECOMING

Wimborne, Major Forster of the Lancers, and Mrs. Forster. (*Acid smile.*) I presume, of course, that Mister Drake will accept them.

ADJUTANT. Quite so. Mister Drake?

DRAKE. (*Rises.*) With pleasure, Mister President.

SENIOR SUBALTERN. Mr. President. (*Hands him paper.*)

ADJUTANT. (*Nods to* SENIOR SUBALTERN.) Thank you.

(SENIOR SUBALTERN *crosses to* DRAKE, *hands him copy, crosses* R. *to his table.*)

DRAKE. Thank you. (*Puts the depositions disinterestedly to one side.*)

SENIOR SUBALTERN. The case for the prosecution is now closed, Mister President.

ADJUTANT. Thank you, Mister Fothergill. (FOTHERGILL *sits.*) Mister Drake.

DRAKE. (*Pause.*) I call (*Rises.*) the Doctor, Mister President.

ADJUTANT. Mister Hutton. (HUTTON *goes to entrance,* U. *door, and ushers* DOCTOR *in.* ADJUTANT *rises.*)

HUTTON. Would you come in, please, Doctor.

DOCTOR. (*Crosses to* R. *of court table. Nervous. They exchange bows.*) Thank you, thank you. (*Bows to* ADJUTANT.)

ADJUTANT. I am sorry that we should have had to recall you, Doctor.

DOCTOR. So am I, Mister President, so am I. But no matter.

ADJUTANT. (*Indicates chair.*) Sir . . . (DOCTOR *sits witness chair,* ADJUTANT *sits.*) Mister Drake . . .

DRAKE. (*Rises.*) Doctor. Two nights ago, I questioned you as to the injuries sustained by Mrs. Hasseltine.

DOCTOR. You did, yes.

DRAKE. Why did you not tell us, Doctor, that she had been attacked with a sword?

DOCTOR. . . . With a sword?

MILLINGTON. A sword . . . ?

ADJUTANT. Be silent, sir. What is this about, Mister Drake?

DRAKE. Mister President. I am prepared to substantiate every single statement I make tonight—however unpleasant—with facts. I take it you will accept factual evidence, Mister President?

DOCTOR. (*Bewildered.*) I do not see how you can prove she was attacked with a sword, Mister Drake—

DRAKE. Then you will have no objection to my trying, sir?

DOCTOR. None whatever . . .

MILLINGTON. (*Rising.*) But I had no sword!

DRAKE. (*Turns to* MILLINGTON.) Trust me. (*Pause. To* ADJUTANT:) Mister President?

ADJUTANT. Very well.

DRAKE. Doctor. Does the name Bandanai mean anything to you? Mrs. Bandanai?

DOCTOR. . . . It does, yes.

DRAKE. Have you recently had occasion to examine her?

DOCTOR. . . . Yes. I have.

DRAKE. Why, Doctor? Because she had been attacked?

DOCTOR. She had been, yes. But—

DRAKE. In what manner, Doctor?

DOCTOR. I cannot answer a question of that kind. It requires a breach of medical ethics.

DRAKE. (*Crosses to* L. *of witness chair.*) Then allow me to make it easy for you, Doctor. (*Crosses to him.*) She was attacked with a sword, was she not?

DOCTOR. . . . It is possible.

DRAKE. Possible? Very well. Let me rephrase my question. She was attacked with a blade, was she not?

DOCTOR. . . . She was, yes—but as I have already said . . .

DRAKE. (*Crosses round to* R. *of him.*) Are you familiar with the expression "making a point," Doctor?

DOCTOR. Naturally I am—yes.

DRAKE. What does it mean?

DOCTOR. It refers to a game that is played in the Mess.
DRAKE. What sort of game?
DOCTOR. The—pursuit of a stuffed pig, or boar.
DRAKE. And what is the object of this game?
DOCTOR. To—pierce the—animal with the point of a sword.
DRAKE. Where, Doctor?
DOCTOR. . . . It is simply to make a hit. I don't think it matters where.
DRAKE. (*Turns to* DOCTOR.) Is it not the object of the exercise to pierce that part of the anatomy which is presented in flight—that is to say, the hind quarters?
DOCTOR. It is—simply an effigy after all, Mister Drake.
DRAKE. Well, where did this game originate, Doctor—in the field?
DOCTOR. I imagine so, yes.
DRAKE. (*Crosses above to* R. *of court table.*) And are those effigies, or living animals?
DOCTOR. But it is—a well-known sport, Mister Drake. It is played all over—
DRAKE. What is a sport, Doctor? To penetrate the anus of a living animal with steel?
DOCTOR. That is a revolting suggestion!
DRAKE. (*Crosses between witness chair and court table.*) It is a revolting game—but that is the Regimental variation, is it not?
ADJUTANT. No, Mister Drake! You will not—
DRAKE. Mister President! Would you care to ask the Doctor where Mrs. Bandanai sustained her injuries?!
DOCTOR. You . . . are not saying . . . ?
DRAKE. I am saying nothing, Doctor, which I do not know and cannot prove to be a fact.
ADJUTANT. Mr. Drake . . .
DRAKE. I am saying, Mister President, that somebody played the Regimental game, with Mrs. Bandanai in the role of pig.
DOCTOR. That is a horrible idea . . .

DRAKE. Yes, Doctor, it is. But were the injuries not consistent with precisely that form of attack?

DOCTOR. (*Horrified.*) I . . .

ADJUTANT. The Court requires an answer to that question, Doctor. (DOCTOR *looks at* ADJUTANT.)

DOCTOR. They would be consistent, yes—

DRAKE. Thank you, Doctor. (*Crosses* L. *to* D. L. *table.*)

DOCTOR. But it never entered my head . . . (*All look at parcel.*)

DRAKE. Now, Doctor, three days ago you examined Mrs. Hasseltine. (*Gets dress out of paper.*)

DOCTOR. There is no connection between the two cases.

DRAKE. None, Doctor?

DOCTOR. Surely not.

DRAKE. (*Swings round, holding dress.*) Do you know what this is?

DOCTOR. It's Mrs. Hasseltine's dress.

DRAKE. Yes, Doctor. The one she was wearing when she was attacked. I got it at the hospital. The Indian woman who was told to burn it thought it too valuable and kept it instead. You see that the skirt is soaked in blood?

DOCTOR. Well, she was cut.

DRAKE. Where, Doctor?

DOCTOR. On the thigh.

DRAKE. High up on the thigh?

DOCTOR. On the thigh, Mister Drake.

DRAKE. (*Crosses to* L. *of witness chair.*) Not on the buttock?

DOCTOR. I have already said . . .

DRAKE. (*Showing skirt to* DOCTOR.) About there?

DOCTOR. Well, yes.

DRAKE. How would you describe that, Doctor?

DOCTOR. . . . It looks like a tear.

DRAKE. A tear? It has absolutely straight, uniform sides, has it not? Is it not a cut—such as might be made by a blade in piercing the material?

DOCTOR. . . . Really, I cannot say.

DRAKE. Doctor . . .

ADJUTANT. (*Rises.*) Let me see the dress.

DRAKE. Yes, Mister President . . . (*Moves upstage, D. end of court table. Hands it to* ADJUTANT.)

MILLINGTON. (*Rises. All look at dress.*) But I didn't attack her with a sword!

DRAKE. Nobody is suggesting that you did.

(ADJUTANT *looks at* DRAKE . . . *then at* MILLINGTON.)

ADJUTANT. (*Examines dress. Turns to* MILLINGTON. *Quieter, but firm.*) Sit down, sir. (MILLINGTON *sits.* ADJUTANT *turns to* DOCTOR, *examines cut for some moments. This is a turning point for him—as* DRAKE *recognises.*) There is no doubt, Doctor, but that this was made with a sword. (*All—slow take on* DOCTOR.)

DOCTOR. I examined the woman, not her clothing. (*Uncomfortable.*) I had no reason to suppose—

DRAKE. Well, now that you have reason to suppose, let me ask you whether the injuries in both cases suggest attempts at the same form of attack—by the same man? (*A pause.*)

DOCTOR. But Mrs. Hasseltine identified her attacker!

DRAKE. And Mrs. Bandanai did not?

DOCTOR. No. No, she didn't.

DRAKE. She has now, Doctor. Now she has. (*A silence.*) Do you still believe that these were two isolated and unconnected attacks?

DOCTOR. No. I would think, now . . . that it is quite possible they were not.

DRAKE. Thank you, Doctor. (*Crosses L. to D. L. table.*)

(*Pause.*)

DOCTOR. But it never entered my head, Mister Drake. I had no reason to doubt Mrs. Hasseltine's word.

DRAKE. (*Turns.*) I know that, Doctor. Now when did you examine Mrs. Bandanai?

DOCTOR. . . . About six months ago. (ADJUTANT *clears dress to his R. and sits.*)

DRAKE. Six months?

DOCTOR. Yes.

DRAKE. You appreciate, of course, that Mister Millington was not here six months ago?

DOCTOR. I do.

DRAKE. So that if these two attacks were made by the same man, it could not have been Mister Millington?

DOCTOR. I realise that now . . .

DRAKE. Thank you, Doctor . . .

ADJUTANT. Mister Drake . . .

DRAKE. (*Crosses* U. L. *of* BOULTON.) Mister President. It is my belief that on the night of the seventeenth, Mrs. Hasseltine was attacked not once, but twice. On the first occasion—if his pathetic attempt to make advances to her can be called an attack—by Mister Millington. And on the second occasion—after he had struck Mister Millington unconscious with the hilt of his sword—by another man. With that same sword. (*All are amazed.*)

ADJUTANT. . . . Who?

DRAKE. Perhaps the Doctor can help us. (*Crosses* R. *above court table to* DOCTOR, R. *of* TRULY.) How did Mrs. Bandanai come to the hospital, Doctor? Was she brought?

DOCTOR. (*Looks at* ADJUTANT.) She was brought. Yes.

DRAKE. (*Crosses to* U. L. *of witness chair.*) By whom? An officer of this Regiment?

DOCTOR. I don't believe I am required to answer that question. (DRAKE *turns to* ADJUTANT.)

ADJUTANT. The Court instructs you to, Doctor.

DOCTOR. Very well— Yes, she was.

DRAKE. By an officer of this Regiment.

DOCTOR. Yes.

DRAKE. Are you prepared to say whom?

DOCTOR. (*Rises.* R. *of witness chair.*) No.

ADJUTANT. (*Rises.*) Doctor . . .

DOCTOR. No, Mr. Harper. You have already far exceeded the limitations of your enquiry into this matter. I shall answer no further questions. (HUTTON *opens*

ACT III   CONDUCT UNBECOMING   105

doors, remains standing. DOCTOR *departs, angry. The* ADJUTANT *stands, deeply shaken. Looks at dress. Slowly sits.*)

ADJUTANT. . . . The Doctor is right, Mister Drake.

DRAKE. (*Crosses to* D. L. *of* ADJUTANT.) Mister President—before you inform the Colonel, as I realise you must—I should be grateful if you would allow me to call the Second in Command, who is waiting to give evidence.

ADJUTANT. . . . He has . . . knowledge of this matter?

DRAKE. He was the last person—to see Mrs. Hasseltine before she was attacked.

ADJUTANT. (*Pause: nods.*) . . . Very well.

DRAKE. (*Crosses* L. *with dress, throws it out arch.*) Thank you, Mister President. (*Sits again.*)

ADJUTANT. Mr. Hutton. (ADJUTANT *nods to* HUTTON. HUTTON *goes off,* R. *They all look changed now, subdued, uncertain.*)

DRAKE. (*Clears paper and string, throws both* L. *arch. Rises.*) Mister President. In questioning the Second in Command, I shall have to begin with a matter which may appear irrelevant to this Court. I should be grateful if you would bear with me. (*Again,* ADJUTANT *nods.* HUTTON *ushers in* ROACH, R. *doors.*)

HUTTON. (*In position.*) Would you come this way, please, sir.

ROACH. (*Enters.*) Thank you, Mister Hutton . . .

ADJUTANT. Good evening, sir. Please be seated.

ROACH. Very well. (*He sits, witness chair.*)

ADJUTANT. Mister Drake. (*Sits.*)

DRAKE. Sir. I should like to ask you about Captain Scarlett.

ROACH. John Scarlett, do you mean?

DRAKE. The officer whose tunic is in that case, yes, sir.

ROACH. What about him, Mister Drake?

DRAKE. How did he die, sir?

ROACH. That is surely a well-known part of the Regiment's history?

DRAKE. . . . I'm afraid I cannot exactly remember the details, sir.

ROACH. Well, you should, Mister Drake, you should.

DRAKE. Yes, sir.

ROACH. Mm. Well . . . John Scarlett, Major Wimborne and I were subalterns together. At the battle of Ratjahpur, John and I were taken prisoner. When he heard about it, Major Wimborne got together a team of volunteers to attempt a rescue. He didn't know that they were holding John and me separately, some two or three hundred yards apart. It so happened, that he came to the place where they were holding me first, and we were able to break out of the rebel position. But when we went on down the line to rescue John, we were too late. He was already dead.

DRAKE. How exactly had he died, sir?

ROACH. He was flayed, Mister Drake, flayed alive.

DRAKE. I see . . .

ROACH. Not a particularly . . . agreeable spectacle.

DRAKE. . . . But he was recognisable, sir?

ROACH. Well . . . the face was terribly distorted, of course. Flaying involves the . . . removal of the skin, as you probably know.

DRAKE. Yes, sir.

ROACH. Then, too, the body had been mutilated. The eyes and tongue had been put out . . . the sex removed.

DRAKE. But it had been . . . Captain John Scarlett?

ROACH. Oh yes. There's no doubt about that whatever.

DRAKE. You saw him with your own eyes, sir?

ROACH. (*All watch* ROACH.) Oh, yes, I saw him.

ADJUTANT. Mister Drake. (*Lifts hand in warning.*)

DRAKE. Yes, Mr. President. I'm sorry, sir.

ROACH. What . . . ? Oh, that's alright, Mr. Drake. Though I'm bound to say, I cannot see how this will help.

DRAKE. I'd like to return now to the night of the seventeenth, sir. (*Picks up notes from* D. L. *table.*) You have stated that you saw Mrs. Hasseltine with Mr. Millington in the Folly and that she broke away from him and began to walk back through the trees towards the Mess.

ROACH. That's right, yes.

DRAKE. What happened then, sir?

ROACH. Well, you know what happened next, Mister Drake.

DRAKE. No, I mean to say, between the time that she broke away from him and when she screamed.

ROACH. (*Puzzled.*) I don't believe that anything happened, Mister Drake.

DRAKE. Well, what did you do, sir? (*Crosses to him.*)

ROACH. Oh, I see. Well, I was anxious to inspect the perimeter piquet, as I told you. They'd been extremely sloppy on the first occasion. It often happens on these ball nights . . .

DRAKE. You went across to inspect them, sir?

ROACH. I did, yes. I'd just about reached them, as far as I can remember . . . Yes, I had, I'd just reached them when the outcry occurred.

DRAKE. You didn't by any chance have Mrs. Hasseltine in view at that moment, did you, sir?

ROACH. No, well, as I said, I hadn't considered the incident sufficiently grave actually to follow her.

DRAKE. What did you do then, sir?

ROACH. I ran towards the Mess.

DRAKE. While you were running, sir, did you see anyone in among the trees—or emerging from the trees, even?

ROACH. (*Sits forward.*) . . . I don't think so . . . Major Wimborne ran past me . . .

DRAKE. Major Wimborne, sir?

ROACH. Yes . . . and Mister Boulton and Mister Winters . . .

DRAKE. Did anyone seem to come from the direction of the trees, sir? Not from the Plain, but from your right?

ROACH. I don't think so, Mister Drake, no and yet . . . Yet curiously enough . . .

DRAKE. . . . Yes, sir?

ROACH. (*Turns body* R.) No, no, it's too absurd . . .

DRAKE. (*Crosses above* R. *of him.*) . . . Well, what is, sir? It may be important.

ROACH. That I doubt. It's simply that . . . when I first went into the trees—when I heard them speaking together . . . I had a curious impression that . . . that I was not alone. That I was being . . . watched by someone else . . .

DRAKE. . . . By another man, do you mean, sir?

ROACH. (*Looks up: smiles.*) It's ridiculous, of course. It often happens at night. You've no idea how many shots are discharged at shadows, Mister Drake.

DRAKE. Yes, sir—but . . . you did get that impression, sir?

ROACH. For a moment, yes. . . . Quite strongly, as a matter of fact. . . .

DRAKE. . . . Have you any idea . . . who it was, sir?

ROACH. (*Smiles.*) It was no one, Mister Drake. It was a shadow, (DRAKE *crosses* C. *below.*) as I say. I shouldn't have mentioned it, but you happened to ask that question.

DRAKE. But you see, sir, it has been established that Mrs. Hasseltine was attacked for a second time that night—

ROACH. For a second time?

DRAKE. Yes, sir. Violently attacked.

ROACH. By Mister Millington, do you mean?

DRAKE. No, sir. By somebody else.

ROACH. By somebody else . . . ? (*Real distress.*)

DRAKE. Yes, sir.

ROACH. (*Real distress for his beloved Regiment: rises.*) Are you sure of this? (*Crosses to him.*)

DRAKE. (*Starts off* L.) I can prove it, sir.

ROACH. But . . . by whom, Mr. Drake?

DRAKE. (*Stops, turns back.*) . . . That has yet to be established, sir.

ROACH. (*Turns, goes up.*) Mr. Harper, has the Colonel been informed of this?

ADJUTANT. (*Rises.*) I am about to tell him, sir.

ROACH. (*Strongly.*) You most certainly should, at once! (*Starts* R., *below witness chair.* COLONEL *enters the Mess. Shock.*)

ADJUTANT. Colonel!

(*All rise.* COLONEL *top step. Pause.* COLONEL *comes forward and looks slowly round. Imperious anger and disappointment.* ROACH *turns* L.)

COLONEL. (*Crosses to* R. *end court table.*) Gentlemen, I enter this Mess—my own Mess—and I find a trial in progress, involving my junior officers, that has gone so far beyond the bounds of reasonable authority in this matter, as to strike at the very heart and centre of this Regiment. You will not need to be told that I am displeased. Displeased, and gravely disappointed. If there is one quality above all others that is the very mark of an officer—and of a gentleman—it is loyalty. Do you understand me, gentlemen? Loyalty.

ALL. Colonel!

COLONEL. (*Crosses* D. C., *turns* U. *to court.*) Very well. You will now return to your quarters. Silently, and at once.

ALL. Colonel!

COLONEL. You, Mister Harper, will remain here. (*Crosses* D. *of court table.*)

ADJUTANT. Colonel.

COLONEL. So will you, Mister Drake.

DRAKE. Colonel.

COLONEL. (*To* D. C., *faces Court.*) The rest of you will report to me, in this Mess, at eight A.M. tomorrow morning. That is all. (*They go, coming to attention: "Colonel."* HART, BOULTON, MILLINGTON *exit* L. *arch.* TRULY, WINTERS, FOTHERGILL *exit* R. *doors. The Court evaporates.* ADJUTANT *crosses* D. R. *to* D. R. *table.*) Lionel—

(*He crosses to* COLONEL.) Would you be good enough to wait in my office. I shall require to speak to you after this.

ROACH. Yes, of course, Colonel. (*Goes,* R. *door,* U. R. *round witness chair, closes doors. A pause.*)

COLONEL. (*Crosses* U. C.) We shall return to your part in this affair in the morning, Mister Harper.

ADJUTANT. Colonel.

COLONEL. (*Turns to* D. R.) I am told, Mister Drake, that you have made an allegation in this room tonight, so . . . gross in detail, so insulting in its implication, that I can hardly believe that I have heard the Doctor correctly.

DRAKE. Colonel—

COLONEL. Be silent, sir. You have been permitted to come to a Regiment of the very highest honour and integrity, Mister Drake. A Regiment whose history and traditions stretch far back into the past—far beyond the life span of any single man. . . . And you have chosen to repay this privilege—with an insult so . . . intolerable, so . . . wounding—

DRAKE. (*Pace forward.*) Permission to speak, Colonel—

COLONEL. No, sir! You have nothing to say to me. I am barely able to bring myself to speak to you . . . (*Turns away* D. R. *one pace.*)

DRAKE. But these are facts, Colonel, which I can prove to be true.

COLONEL. You cannot prove an impossibility.

DRAKE. I am sorry, Colonel, but—

COLONEL. No, sir! There is—no officer in this Regiment—capable of . . . such an act. (*Is struggling to reject something which strikes at the basic premiss of his whole life.*)

ADJUTANT. (*One big step to* R. C.) Colonel . . .

COLONEL. No, sir!

DRAKE. I beg you to ask the Adjutant, Colonel—

COLONEL. I am no better pleased with the Adjutant than I am with yourself in this affair.
ADJUTANT. With your permission, Colonel.
COLONEL. Well?
ADJUTANT. I know that I am justly rebuked . . .
COLONEL. You are, sir.
ADJUTANT. But I cannot in honour say other than that I believe Mister Drake to be right in this affair.

(*Pause.* COLONEL *is shocked.*)

COLONEL. . . . What did you say?
ADJUTANT. There are certain facts, Colonel, which cannot be denied.
COLONEL. (*Breaks to* ADJUTANT.) Facts?
ADJUTANT. Yes, Colonel.
COLONEL. You speak to me of facts?
ADJUTANT. But I am convinced, Colonel, that Mrs. Hasseltine's dress was cut with a sword—
COLONEL. I am not speaking of dresses—
ADJUTANT. —And the Doctor has given evidence that Mrs. Bandanai was attacked.

(*Pause.* COLONEL *knows this to be true. And the fact that it was hidden from him.*)

COLONEL. (*Turns* U. R. *of court table.*) . . . That is a matter that will be looked into.
DRAKE. With respect, Colonel, when did you first hear of the attack on Mrs. Bandanai?
COLONEL. . . . That is no concern of yours.
DRAKE. (*Hating to do this.*) But if you have already been—lied to once, Colonel—
COLONEL. (*Fast turn to* DRAKE. *Crosses to* C.) I have not been lied to! We do not—lie to one another in this Mess! Gentlemen do not question the honour of other gentlemen, Mr. Drake! (*Comes* D. C.)
DRAKE. He will attack again, Colonel.

COLONEL. (*Pause.*) . . . What?

DRAKE. (*Crosses D. L. C. level with* ADJUTANT.) I am convinced that a man who has already attacked twice will attack for a third time, Colonel. And there are ladies here who need your protection.

COLONEL. . . . You have not convinced me . . . that this is the work of one man . . . least of all an officer of this Regiment.

DRAKE. I believe that I can prove it, with your permission, Colonel.

COLONEL. . . . How?

DRAKE. By recalling Mrs. Hasseltine to the witness chair, Colonel.

COLONEL. . . . You are suggesting that I should allow this trial to continue?

DRAKE. . . . I am suggesting, with respect, Colonel, that I can best serve you and this Regiment by examining the matter here—where I alone shall suffer if I am mistaken—rather than in the public forum to which you would be compelled, Colonel. (*Crosses U. to C. of court table.* COLONEL *looks at him. Pause.*)

COLONEL. (*Turns D.*) You are saying that you are prepared to stake your honour on this?

DRAKE. I have no other means of retrieving myself before you, and before this Regiment.

COLONEL. I see. (*Pause.*) And you, Mister Harper? Are you willing to stake twelve years of service on the outcome of this trial?

ADJUTANT. (*Pause.*) I must abide by what I have said to you, Colonel.

COLONEL. Very well, gentlemen, you leave me no alternative. I give you twenty-four hours in which to prove your theories correct. Should you fail, you will not expect to remain with this Regiment. I shall myself be present. Tomorrow night. (*Slight pause.*) Good night to you. (*Goes, R. doors.*)

ADJUTANT. Good night, Colonel. (*A pause.* HARPER

gathers his papers from court table, turns to go, stops, turns to DRAKE.) We have hurt a man whom I greatly admire.

DRAKE. I do not know how we can fail to go on doing so.

ADJUTANT. I trust you are aware that I knew nothing of this.

DRAKE. . . . I am . . . yes. Thank you for supporting me, Mister Harper.

ADJUTANT. It is necessary, at all times, to support the honour of the Regiment.

DRAKE. . . . Yes.

ADJUTANT. Well . . . I will say good night to you.

DRAKE. Good night, sir.

ADJUTANT. Good night. (*Goes,* R. *doors.*)

(DRAKE, *grim, tired, crosses after a moment to stare into* SCARLETT *tunic showcase. A thought occurs to him. Turns slowly, stares at dress on Defence table. Crosses, takes up dress. Sees depositions; crumples them as he walks off . . . LIGHTS DOWN, AND UP . . .*)

ACT THREE

SCENE 2

The Mess. The next night. They enter U. R. *veranda to* C. *arch,* ROACH *first.*

WIMBORNE. (*Crosses* D. R. *corner court table.*) Lionel, forget about it, stop worrying.

ROACH. (*Crosses* D. L. *of court, sits* DRAKE'S *chair.*) I can't. This is a wretched business, Alastair, and . . . and getting wholly out of hand. Besides, I feel responsible.

WIMBORNE. (*Takes cup off caraje.*) You, why?

ROACH. If only I had dealt with the matter at the time.

WIMBORNE. (*Drinks water.*) I swear to God, Lionel, you'd find a way to blame yourself for everything that happens in this Regiment. (*Crosses to* L. *corner court table.*)

ROACH. In any case, this kind of trial is a terrible mistake. And now the Colonel has involved himself personally. I'm going to tell him what I think. (*Starts* R.)

WIMBORNE. Lionel, wait! (ROACH *stops.*) Take my advice. This is not the moment, you can only make matters worse. See what happens tonight.

ROACH. Alright, Alastair, if that's what you think.

WIMBORNE. (*Crosses to him.*) I do.

ROACH. It's almost midnight. I'd better fetch him. (*Doesn't.*)

WIMBORNE. Go on, then . . . and, Lionel, (ROACH *stops on steps* R.) stop worrying.

(ROACH *goes,* R. *doors.* MRS. HASSELTINE *comes onto veranda,* U. L. *arch.*)

MRS. HASSELTINE. Alastair . . . Alastair . . . (*Crosses to* L. *of court table.*)

WIMBORNE. (*Going up. Crosses to meet her.*) What are you doing here?

MRS. HASSELTINE. I must speak with you. (*The whole scene made doubly urgent by need for quietness.*)

WIMBORNE. What the devil's the matter? You shouldn't be here.

MRS. HASSELTINE. I've been called again for tonight.

WIMBORNE. So have I. (*Turns away* R.)

MRS. HASSELTINE. You?

WIMBORNE. . . . Yes.

MRS. HASSELTINE. Then they must know . . .

WIMBORNE. (*Turns to her.*) Oh, for God's sake . . .

MRS. HASSELTINE. But they must, Alastair! (*Crosses* D. L. C.)

WIMBORNE. (*Crosses to her.*) Listen to me! Nobody knows anything! Nobody will discover anything! Just so long as you remain silent. (*Crosses away from her. Pause.*)

MRS. HASSELTINE. I don't know that I am any longer prepared to.

WIMBORNE. What the hell does that mean?

MRS. HASSELTINE. I have been humiliated once because of you, Alastair. I do not intend to be humiliated again! (*Crosses R. of C.*)

WIMBORNE. Listen to me, Marge! You are the last person here who can afford to tell the truth! Remember that!

MRS. HASSELTINE. (*Turns to him.*) Oh! What does that mean?

WIMBORNE. You owe us everything, Marge! Your house, your servants, your land; everything. Without this Regiment, you are nothing.

MRS. HASSELTINE. (*Starts* U. R.) . . . I see. Thank you for reminding me of my place in this community.

WIMBORNE. (*Crosses to her.*) Marge, you know damn well . . .

MRS. HASSELTINE. And in your estimation. (*Exits veranda* U. R.)

WIMBORNE. Marge!

COLONEL. (*Off.*) Very well, gentlemen. I am ready.

(WIMBORNE *goes via* U. L. *veranda, she via veranda* R. *The* COLONEL *comes on, crosses to* D. R. *armchair, sits with* ROACH *and* DOCTOR *going straight to extra chairs* U. L., *sit.* DRAKE *and* MILLINGTON *enter arch* L. DRAKE *again carries wrapped package.* DRAKE, MILLINGTON *take places. The Court files on as before but much slower and quieter.* HUTTON *closes doors.* ADJUTANT *last to his place. A silence.*)

ADJUTANT. Be seated, gentlemen. (*They sit.*) This Court is now in session. Mister Drake.

DRAKE. (*Rises.*) I call Mrs. Hasseltine, Mister President.

ADJUTANT. Mister Hutton.

HUTTON. Yes, sir. . . . Would you come in, please, ma'am.

(HUTTON *"Sir," goes off. Dead silence. Slightly extended wait. He returns with* MRS. HASSELTINE. ADJUTANT *alone rises. She looks at assembled Regiment. They half rise and sit. She notes it.*)

ADJUTANT. Be seated, ma'am, please. . . .

MRS. HASSELTINE. . . . Thank you. (*She sits. Bows to* COLONEL *who looks stonily.*)

ADJUTANT. (*Sits,* HUTTON *closes doors.*) Mister Drake . . .

DRAKE. (*Rises.*) Mrs. Hasseltine. When I questioned you earlier, you told me that you had been attacked by Mister Millington—that you had struck him down with . . . something—and that you had then run into this Mess for fear he might attack you again.

MRS. HASSELTINE. Yes.

DRAKE. Is there anything you wish to add to that statement, ma'am?

MRS. HASSELTINE. No.

DRAKE. Is there anything you wish to retract from it?

MRS. HASSELTINE. No.

DRAKE. You are certain?

MRS. HASSELTINE. I am.

DRAKE. . . . Very well. (DRAKE *leans down front of* D. L. *table, where he has placed dress. He holds it out, turns to her.*) Do you recognize this, ma'am? (*It is a tremendous shock to her. She stares at it.*) Yes. The Indian woman thought it too valuable to burn. (*Extends skirt, moves* D. L. C.) I would like you to look at the skirt, ma'am. (*She stares at it. Jerks her head round to look up at the Court.*) I have already explained to the Court the significance of this sword-cut, Mrs. Hasseltine.

MRS. HASSELTINE. . . . I don't understand you.

DRAKE. Very well. (*Puts dress on table, goes close to her.*) Would you please look behind you, Mrs. Hasseltine.

MRS. HASSELTINE. . . . What?

DRAKE. (D. L. C.) Turn around. Look behind you.

MRS. HASSELTINE. . . . Why?

DRAKE. Are you afraid to? (*Very slowly, she turns* L. *There is something creepy about this.* . . .) What do you see, Mrs. Hasseltine?

MRS. HASSELTINE. (*Mystified.*) . . . The Plain.

DRAKE. And further to your left?

MRS. HASSELTINE. . . . The Court.

DRAKE. And again further . . . ?

MRS. HASSELTINE. (*Turns in her chair.*) . . . A wall.

DRAKE. What else, Mrs. Hasseltine? (*Pause.*) Well . . . ?

MRS. HASSELTINE. . . . A showcase.

DRAKE. What is in the showcase?

MRS. HASSELTINE. . . . A tunic.

DRAKE. Whose, Mrs. Hasseltine? (*She makes a gesture, almost weary, of putting her hand to her head. Lowering it, she turns slowly to* DRAKE.)

MRS. HASSELTINE. (*Turns to* DRAKE.) . . . You know?

DRAKE. (*Gently. Crosses to her.*) Yes, ma'am. I know who was there that night. . . . (*She lowers her head, turns* R. *He throws dress in* U. R. *corner.*) I have no wish to distress you, Mrs. Hasseltine. (*Crosses above to* R. *of her.*) I simply want you to tell us the truth. Will you do that, ma'am?

MRS. HASSELTINE. (*Nods.*) . . . Yes.

DRAKE. Were you attacked by Captain Scarlett?

MRS. HASSELTINE. (*Reaction.*) . . . Yes, I was.

DRAKE. I am sorry, ma'am. . . .

COLONEL. (*Jumps up, crosses* L. *to* C., *stops.*) Mister Drake . . .

DRAKE. With respect, Colonel, I believe that all will

become plain in a moment or two. If you will permit me to continue.

COLONEL. Very well. (*Crosses to* DRAKE's *chair, facing off* L.)

DRAKE. . . . I must ask you first, ma'am, whether Mister Millington attacked you in any serious sense at all?

MRS. HASSELTINE. (*Almost amused.*) He hasn't the . . . violence in him, Mister Drake.

DRAKE. He did not assault, or . . . ?

MRS. HASSELTINE. He begged me to cry out. He begged me to accuse him.

DRAKE. Do you still wish to bring a complaint against him?

MRS. HASSELTINE. Of what? Inherent gentleness?

DRAKE. That, surely, is no crime.

MRS. HASSELTINE. *You think not*, Mister Drake? Then you are in the wrong place. He is the only gentle man I have met in all my years with this Regiment.

DRAKE. You withdraw the charge before this Court against him?

MRS. HASSELTINE. I do, yes.

DRAKE. You make no complaint of any kind?

MRS. HASSELTINE. None whatever.

DRAKE. (*Crosses* U. *to* L. *of witness chair.*) Thank you, ma'am. I must now ask you about the night of the seventeenth. . . . (COLONEL *faces* MRS. HASSELTINE.)

MRS. HASSELTINE. He came—so suddenly. Out of the darkness. My name. And then . . . No face. The lights on the Plain. No face. . . . (*Absolutely still, calm.*)

DRAKE. He had a sword?

MRS. HASSELTINE. I tried to run. But I fell. He . . . He cut me. And then . . . he said . . .

DRAKE. . . . What did he say, ma'am?

MRS. HASSELTINE. He *laughed* and said . . . "A point, Marge. A veritable point. . . ." (*Covers her face with one hand—not weeping. The* COLONEL *sits in* DRAKE's *chair.*)

DRAKE. I am sorry to persist in these questions, ma'am. But you have only to tell us who he was. . . .

MRS. HASSELTINE. I don't know who he was. . . .

DRAKE. But you must, ma'am. . . .

MRS. HASSELTINE. I don't, Mister Drake. . . .

DRAKE. Then why did you accuse Mister Millington, ma'am?

MRS. HASSELTINE. I had to do something. (*Turns away* R.)

DRAKE. (*Crosses below to* R. *of her.*) Why, Mrs. Hasseltine? Unless you recognised your attacker and knew that you could never accuse that man?

MRS. HASSELTINE. I only knew . . .

DRAKE. What Major Wimborne chose to tell you?

MRS. HASSELTINE. I have nothing to say. Nothing!

DRAKE. (*Kneels at witness chair.*) But . . . his voice, ma'am. You must have recognised his voice.

MRS. HASSELTINE. It was the voice of John Scarlett . . .

DRAKE. But—

MRS. HASSELTINE. (*Rises* L. *of witness chair.*) Don't you understand, Mister Drake? It doesn't matter which one of these men it was. They are all the same. Stupid, cruel men, who treat—pigs and women—as though they were . . . objects. . . .

COLONEL. (*Rises.*) Mrs. Hasseltine, you are overwrought.

MRS. HASSELTINE. (*Crosses to* COLONEL.) Colonel. Do you not yet know what you are sire to? They are all John Scarlett. Every one of them.

COLONEL. That will be all, ma'am.

MRS. HASSELTINE. Yes. (*Nods, starts* R.) Oh, yes. (*Crosses to exit* U. C. *veranda.*) It has taken me too long to accept what I have always known. You are scum. (*Goes, veranda* L. *Silence.*)

COLONEL. Mister Drake. Explain.

DRAKE. (*Rises, breaks* D. *of witness chair. At attention.*) Colonel, there is an officer in this Regiment, who dresses in the uniform worn by this Regiment until shortly after the Mutiny; and in that fashion attacks women.

COLONEL. You must be mistaken.

DRAKE. It is a fact, Colonel. As you have just heard confirmed by Mrs. Hasseltine.

COLONEL. Nobody dressed in that manner on the night of the seventeenth.

DRAKE. No, Colonel.

COLONEL. Well, then?

DRAKE. It appears that it is not always necessary.

COLONEL. For what?

DRAKE. The impersonation.

COLONEL. Why would anyone want to impersonate John Scarlett?

DRAKE. (*Crosses* L. *to* C.) With your permission, Colonel, I should like to ask Major Wimborne.

COLONEL. (*Pause.*) Very well. Call him. (*Crosses* R., *sits* D. R. *chair.*)

ADJUTANT. Mister Boulton.

(*Silence.* BOULTON *goes, returns* L. *arch with* WIMBORNE, *belligerent, uncertain what* MRS. HASSELTINE *has said.*)

BOULTON. Would you come this way, please, sir?

WIMBORNE. About bloody time, too. (WIMBORNE *moves in, stops* L. *corner court table.*) Colonel, sir.

ADJUTANT. Be seated, sir, please.

WIMBORNE. Alright. (*Crosses* R. *to witness chair. Sits —a sigh.*) Well?

DRAKE. (*Is not impressed by anger—he is as coldly angry himself.*) Major Wimborne, sir. What happened to Mrs. Bandanai?

WIMBORNE. How the hell would I know?

DRAKE. (*Turns front.*) Six months ago, Mrs. Bandanai was attacked in a particular manner and it was you who took her to the hospital.

WIMBORNE. (*Drily.*) Oh, really?

DRAKE. (*Breaks towards him.*) You were seen, sir.
WIMBORNE. By whom?
DRAKE. The orderlies on duty.
WIMBORNE. I see, wogs. . . .
DRAKE. And by the Doctor.
WIMBORNE. Did he tell you that?
DRAKE. Do you deny it?
WIMBORNE. Why should I deny it?
DRAKE. You did take her to the hospital, then?
WIMBORNE. Alright,—yes, yes, I did.
DRAKE. (*Front.*) How did it come about?
WIMBORNE. I found her.
DRAKE. Where, sir?
WIMBORNE. What the devil does it matter where?
DRAKE. In your bungalow, sir? (*Slight pause.*) Is that where you found her?
WIMBORNE. . . . What if I did?
DRAKE. How did she come to be there?
WIMBORNE. I haven't the faintest idea.
DRAKE. (*Turns to him.*) Had you not asked her to spend the evening with you?
WIMBORNE. . . . That's no crime.
DRAKE. I didn't say it was, sir.
WIMBORNE. (*Looks at* COLONEL.) Alright, yes. Yes, I did.

(COLONEL *dead pan.*)

DRAKE. Then how did you come to "find" her, sir? Had you gone out for a walk?
WIMBORNE. I'd been down to the piquets.
DRAKE. The piquets?
WIMBORNE. I was Officer of the Week.
DRAKE. I see. And when you came back, you "found" that she'd been attacked?
WIMBORNE. Yes. Yes, she had.
DRAKE. How, sir? In what way?
WIMBORNE. I don't know. I wasn't there.

DRAKE. Was she bleeding, sir?
WIMBORNE. There was blood on the floor, yes.
DRAKE. Where was she bleeding from?
WIMBORNE. I don't know. I didn't examine her. I took her straight to the hosptial. (*Slight pause.*)
DRAKE. Did you report this attack to the Colonel, sir?
WIMBORNE. (*Looks at* COLONEL.) . . . No.
DRAKE. Why not?
WIMBORNE. I didn't think it necessary. There seemed no point in . . . making trouble . . . for some . . .
DRAKE. Wog?
WIMBORNE. Yes.
DRAKE. And so by avoiding trouble then, you made it later instead.
WIMBORNE. What are you talking about?
DRAKE. You are surely aware that Mrs. Hasseltine has been attacked?
WIMBORNE. That's a different thing entirely.
DRAKE. I don't think so, sir. Neither does the Doctor. Nor does Mrs. Hasseltine herself.
WIMBORNE. I don't believe you.
DRAKE. They have both given evidence before this court, sir. Mrs. Hasseltine went further. She identified her attacker.
WIMBORNE. Yes! Mister Millington.
DRAKE. No, sir. Captain John Scarlett.
WIMBORNE. That's ridiculous! John Scarlett is dead!
DRAKE. I don't think so, sir.
WIMBORNE. Well, I ought to know! I brought in his remains myself!
DRAKE. Yes, sir. Yes, you did.
WIMBORNE. . . . Well, then!
DRAKE. (*Crosses above to* R. *of him and* D.) I have been asking myself, sir, what manner of man could have been responsible for attacks of this kind. I would say it was the work of a sportsman, wouldn't you? A man who enjoys his sport?
WIMBORNE. Why ask me?

DRAKE. Well, who is the champion at "Making a Point" in this Mess, sir?

WIMBORNE. There is no champion.

DRAKE. (*Crosses U. of witness chair to L. C.*) The acknowledged master, then. The outstanding sportsman. The man who scored two goals against the Lancers in the final chukka?

WIMBORNE. That was me.

DRAKE. (*Turns to him.*) Exactly, sir. Indeed it would be fair to say that you epitomise everything that is most admired in this Regiment. You are aggressive, bold, fearless . . . (*Crosses to* WIMBORNE.)

WIMBORNE. (*Astonished amusement.*) You don't think I did it?

DRAKE. Why not, sir?

WIMBORNE. Not me?

DRAKE. I should be interested to hear your reasoning, sir. (*Crosses to D. L. table. But* WIMBORNE *throws his head back and roars with laughter, real, free laughter.*) I'm glad you find it amusing, sir.

WIMBORNE. (*Laughing.*) Why don't you examine your own evidence, laddie?

DRAKE. . . . What?

WIMBORNE. (*Enjoying himself hugely.*) I was right, smack, bang in the middle of the Plain when Marjorie was attacked! I was dancing with Mrs. Forster! Everybody saw me!

DRAKE. I don't believe you!

WIMBORNE. (*Points.*) Well, ask him. Ask Fothergill. He took the depositions. It's all written down!

DRAKE. But that can't be true.

WIMBORNE. (*Turns.*) Or Mister Harper—ask him.

ADJUTANT. Mister Fothergill?

SENIOR SUBALTERN. (*Rises.*) It's true, Mister Harper. I saw Major Wimborne myself. (DRAKE *breaks D.*) And both Mrs. Forster and the Doctor have sworn to it in their depositions . . .

WIMBORNE. (*Laughing.*) Well? Any more bright ideas? Laddie! (*A silence.* DRAKE *is stunned.*)

DRAKE. But . . . if it wasn't you . . .

WIMBORNE. Who was it, then? Major Roach? Um? (FOTHERGILL *sits.*)

DRAKE. He was inspecting the piquet . . .

WIMBORNE. That's right, I saw him! I ran right past him! Well, what about the *Doctor*, then?

DRAKE. He was with Major Forster . . .

WIMBORNE. And I was with Mrs. Forster. So you're right back where you started! Aren't you?

DRAKE. I don't understand . . . (*Pause.*)

WIMBORNE. We seem to have run out of officers.

DRAKE. (*Quietly: to* WIMBORNE.) You know, sir.

WIMBORNE. What . . . ?

DRAKE. You know who Captain Scarlett is.

WIMBORNE. He's dead.

DRAKE. Sir, if you do nothing, this man will attack again.

WIMBORNE. (*Slightest hesitation.*) Then I must remember to stand with my back to the wall, mustn't I?

DRAKE. (*Fast cross to him.*) Sir!

WIMBORNE. (*Rises,* R. *witness chair. Shouts him down.*) I cannot help you, Mister Drake. (*Crosses* R. *and* U. *to steps.*)

DRAKE. (*Turns to* ADJUTANT.) Mister President, I wish to recall the Second in Command.

ADJUTANT. Why?

DRAKE. Because he was the last one to see Mrs. Hasseltine before she was attacked . . . there is something here that I have missed. . . . The man that he almost saw . . .

ROACH. (*Rises, breaks* D. *slightly.*) That was just an impression, Mister Drake.

DRAKE. It is all that we have got, sir.

ADJUTANT. Colonel . . . ?

COLONEL. (*Sitting like a stone.*) Let him.

ROACH. (*Rises. Crosses to witness chair, sits.*) Very well, Colonel.

ADJUTANT. Thank you, Major Wimborne.

WIMBORNE. (*Turns to* COLONEL.) I am sorry, Colonel. There is nothing further that I can tell this Court. (*Crosses u. steps.*)

COLONEL. Do not go far, Alastair. (WIMBORNE *stops.*)

WIMBORNE. No, Colonel. (*Goes,* R. *doors, closes them.*)

ADJUTANT. Mr. Drake.

(ROACH *moves to the witness chair. Sits.*)

DRAKE. (*Crosses to* L. *of witness chair.*) Sir, I want to go back to that moment when you entered the Folly . . .

ROACH. (*Nods.*) Very well.

DRAKE. Now it is dark. . . . You have just sent Mister Hart to inspect the native quarters. . . . The orchestra is playing on the Plain. . . . You hear voices . . . Mister Millington pleading, Mrs. Hasseltine angry. . . . You step in among the trees . . .

ROACH. Yes . . .

DRAKE. You can't see anything clearly . . .

ROACH. No, I can't.

DRAKE. But there is someone . . . very close to you, sir . . . you can sense him . . . you can feel him watching you. . . .

ROACH. (*Nods.*) I can, yes . . .

DRAKE. Where is he, sir . . . ? Where is he?

ROACH. He is . . . behind me. . . .

DRAKE. So you turn . . .

(ROACH *half turns. Pause.*)

ROACH. So I— It's no use, Mister Drake. I can see no one.

DRAKE. Think, sir. Think!

ROACH. . . . It was just an impression . . .

DRAKE. No, sir, it was a real person, sir. . . . It was Captain Scarlett. . . .

ROACH. I am sorry, Mister Drake. . . .

(DRAKE *bows his head in defeat and turns away.*)

DRAKE. (*Slow cross to* D. L. *table.*) I see, well . . . thank you, sir. Thank you. (*Turns to* ROACH.)

ROACH. I am sorry, Mister Drake. I realise now how close I must have come to seeing him.

DRAKE. (*Tired smile.*) We are all close to doing that, sir. (*Looks at showcase.*) But not quite close enough.

ADJUTANT. . . . Have you any further questions, Mister Drake?

DRAKE. No, Mister President. (*Comes to attention.*) I am sorry, Colonel. I have failed you.

COLONEL. (*Rises. Tragic dignity.*) No, Mister Drake. You have failed neither me nor yourself. Be seated, please. (*Crosses to court table. Sits. From now on the stricken figure of the* COLONEL *dominates the scene.* ROACH *rises.* DRAKE *sits his chair.*) Lionel, would you be good enough to send Major Wimborne to me, please?

ROACH. Colonel. (*Goes,* R. *doors.* DRAKE *sits, defeated. He does not then move.*)

COLONEL. (*Crosses to* R. *of court table.*) Mister Harper. The purpose of this Court is to pronounce on the guilt or otherwise of Mister Millington. In view of the fact that the charge against him has been withdrawn, that will not long delay you. Proceed. (*Crosses* D. *to* D. R. *table.*)

ADJUTANT. I can only advise you, gentlemen, to vote not guilty. Mister Truly.

TRULY. Not guilty, Mister President.

ADJUTANT. Mister Winters.

WINTERS. Not guilty.

ADJUTANT. Mister Hart.

HART. Not guilty.

ADJUTANT. Mister Boulton.

BOULTON. Not guilty.

ADJUTANT. (*Rises.*) The President also votes not guilty. (*Rises.*) Mr. Millington, rise, please. (MILLING-

TON *stands*.) You have been found not guilty by this Court. You are cleared absolutely as to honour and integrity. You are free to return to your duties. This Court is dissolved. (*All rise.*)

COLONEL. (*Crosses* D. R. *level with* MILLINGTON.) Mister Millington. You have been unjustly treated by this Regiment. You have yourself behaved with some stupidity. I trust we may now see a new beginning.

MILLINGTON. . . . Yes, Colonel.

COLONEL. (*Nods.*) Very well. I welcome you to this Regiment.

MILLINGTON. Thank you, Colonel. (*A pause. The* COLONEL *turns away.*)

ADJUTANT. (*Rises. Crosses round* R. *of court table and down to* MILLINGTON.) I congratulate you, Mister Millington. (*General congratulations.* MILLINGTON *crosses* R. *to* L. *of* C.)

COLONEL. Leave us now, (*As* FOTHERGILL *shakes his hand.*) please, gentlemen. Mister Drake, you will remain . . .

(ALLS *"Colonel . . . Good night, Colonel . . ." etc. As they leave they cluster round* MILLINGTON, *shaking his hand, congratulating him.* BOULTON *crosses* D. L. *of* MILLINGTON *and shakes hands.* HART *crosses* U. L. *of* MILLINGTON *and shakes hands.* TRULY *crosses* R. *of* MILLINGTON *and shakes hands.* WINTERS *crosses above* MILLINGTON *and shakes hands.* FOTHERGILL *crosses* L. *to* R. *of him and shakes hands.*)

HART. Come over to my quarters and we'll celebrate . . .

ADJUTANT. (*Has crossed* U. *to veranda top* C.) Quietly, gentlemen.

(*They turn and start* R. MILLINGTON *hangs back at witness chair.* FOTHERGILL *crosses to* D. *end* R. *steps.*

Truly *crosses to* U. *end* R. *steps.* Winters *crosses to top step.* Hart *crosses to* U. *end step.* Boulton *crosses to* D. *second step.*)

Millington. (*At attention.*) With your permission, Colonel.
Colonel. Very well.
Millington. (*Crosses to* Drake.) Thank you, Arthur.
Drake. (*A look at him, then front.*) You have nothing to thank me for.
Millington. I have a bourgeois principle to thank you for. (*They smile and shake hands.*) We may see you later, then?
Drake. Perhaps.
Millington. Good night, Arthur.
Drake. Good night, Millington.
Millington. (*Crosses* C. *at attention.*) Colonel.
Colonel. Mister Millington.
Hart. Come on, old man.

(*The* Subalterns *exit, ad libs, taking* Millington.)

Adjutant. (*Crosses* D. *from veranda to* L. *of witness chair.*) I am sorry, Colonel. . . .
Colonel. (D. R. *at* D. R. *table.*) No, Mister Harper. You have behaved as I should expect you to. With exemplary courage and fairness. You have done well.
Adjutant. . . . I would that we had done less well. Good night, Colonel.
Colonel. Good night . . .

(Ajutant *looks at* Drake, *then leaves,* R. *doors.*)

Drake. (R *of* D. L. *table,* U. *end.*) . . . I, too, take little pleasure in what I have done, Colonel.
Colonel. You have done what needed to be done. (*Slight pause.*) I have this morning received your letter of resignation. Do you wish me to accept it, Mister Drake, or to tear it up?

DRAKE. I should like you to accept it. I am sorry, Colonel. I find that I cannot . . . put my honour onto a Regiment. Or onto a man. It is what I am . . . what I do.

COLONEL. In a Regiment, it is necessary to hold one's honour in trust.

DRAKE. I understand that, Colonel.

COLONEL. (*Crosses* U.) Very well. I accept your letter of resignation, Mister Drake. (*Goes to veranda.*) With regret. (DRAKE *hesitates.* WIMBORNE *enters* R. *doors, crosses* D. R. *of witness chair. The* COLONEL *sees him and dismisses* DRAKE. *Turns to him.*) Good night, Mr. Drake . . . and thank you.

DRAKE. Good night, Colonel. (*Goes.*)

COLONEL. (*Turns to him.*) Alastair!

WIMBORNE. I couldn't tell you, Ben. You would have been obliged to take official action. The Regiment could never have survived the scandal. What we have hidden has been hidden too long.

COLONEL. (D. *one step.*) . . . I want the matter ended now.

WIMBORNE. Very well. Then leave it to me. It is a matter of honour. It will be settled in the traditional manner. (*Pause.*)

COLONEL. . . . A matter of honour.

WIMBORNE. It is not as you think, Ben.

COLONEL. Oh, yes. I am the Regiment. What I have allowed to happen is what I am. (*Slight pause.*) It is as well my time here is nearly done. You will not again speak to me of honour. (*Exits,* L. *arch.*)

(WIMBORNE *pats holster, crosses* D. C., *says "Oh, God"— runs to wall lamp,* L. C. *arch, turns it down. Looks out into night, runs out.* WIMBORNE *returns from veranda with pressing urgency.*)

WIMBORNE (*Crossing* D. R. *to* D. R. *table. Calls.*) Pradah Singh! (WIMBORNE *moves table to* R. *arm of witness chair, brings* D. R. *armchair to behind table, gets table lamp from steps* R. *behind wall, puts it on table.* PRADAH SINGH *comes on,* R. *doors, crosses* D. *off bottom step.*)

PRADAH. Sahib?

WIMBORNE. Get these lamps out. Quickly.

(PRADAH SINGH *begins to go round room, turning down lamps,* L. *wall lamp,* R. C. *wall lamp, and* U. R. *wall lamp.* WIMBORNE *takes gun from holster, puts on table, gets bullets from pocket, puts on table.*)

PRADAH. . . . Is there anything further, sahib?

WIMBORNE. (*Sits behind table.*) No, just don't come back, that's all.

PRADAH. . . . No, sahib. (*Goes, closing* R. *doors.*)

(WIMBORNE *breaks barrel of gun, looks through it.* DRAKE *enters in the shadows,* L. *arch,* D.)

DRAKE. (*Crosses to* C.) . . . What are you going to do?

(WIMBORNE *looks up. Pauses. Loads gun.*)

WIMBORNE. (*Loading.*) You've been very anxious to meet Captain Scarlett, Mister Drake. Now you shall.

DRAKE. . . . What?

WIMBORNE. He's out there now. When I turn down this lamp, he'll come in.

DRAKE. (*Stares at gun.*) But why?

WIMBORNE. Because he always does. We talk together, Mister Drake. He likes to have someone to talk to. (*Locks barrel, puts gun* D. *on table.*)

DRAKE. But you can't . . .

WIMBORNE. You're keen on telling us what we can and can't do, aren't you, Mister Drake? And you know nothing. Nothing!

DRAKE. (*A step in.*) But . . .
WIMBORNE. No! (*Puts down the gun. Intense bright MOONLIGHT on the veranda, falling from back towards stage.*) You think this is just a matter of honour, don't you?
DRAKE. . . . Isn't it?
WIMBORNE. No, Mr. Drake, it is not. (*Rises, crosses to* DRAKE.) It is a matter of comradeship, friendship. (*Looks towards veranda—turns down table lamp.*) Now you wait in there. (*Points to* L. *arch.*) You can watch, if you wish. But you will not intervene. Do you understand me?
DRAKE. But, sir . . . !
WIMBORNE. Be quiet! Look, just do as you're told!

(*A VOICE beyond the moonlight. One we have not heard.* CAPTAIN SCARLETT.)

SCARLETT. Alastair! Are you there, you old rogue?!

(DRAKE *turns* U. *towards sound.*)

WIMBORNE. (*Starts* R.) Get in there—quickly!
DRAKE. But . . . !
WIMBORNE. (*Crosses to below* D. R. *table, picks up gun.*) Get in there!

(DRAKE *is forced just inside card room doorway.* WIMBORNE *crosses to table with lamp and gun. SILENCE. INTENSE MOONLIGHT. An approach. Booted feet on the veranda. A commanding, faceless figure steps into view. The bright moonlight, coming from behind, hides his face. The voice is amused, harsh.*)

SCARLETT. Alastair, are you there?
WIMBORNE. I'm here, John.
SCARLETT. (*Entering. Stands top step,* C. *arch.*) Well, turn up the lamp, you silly bugger. (WIMBORNE *turns up*

lamp. SCARLETT *has the face—but only the face—of* LIONEL ROACH. WIMBORNE *has gun behind his back.*) That's better. Now we can see what we're doing. (SCARLETT *crosses to showcase, opens it to take out and put on uniform jacket.*)

WIMBORNE. (*Crosses* L. *to* D. L. *table.*) You won't be needing the jacket tonight, John. You won't be going anywhere tonight.

SCARLETT. (*Crosses* D., *putting on tunic.*) Why not? Because of that little swine Lionel Roach? That was a close call, when he started talking about the man he almost saw. (*Fiercely.*) Well, no matter! I'm getting stronger, Alastair. . . . I've almost taken over from the little runt once for all. . . . (*Crosses to* D. R. *table, draws sword.*)

WIMBORNE. That's why we must be rid of you now.

SCARLETT. What . . . ?

(WIMBORNE *fires. The case shatters. The dummy plunges out.* SCARLETT *drops sword, jerks as though shocked, puts hand to head in confusion, becomes* ROACH *again, looks at* WIMBORNE, *recognises him.*)

ROACH. (*Puzzled.*) Alastair?

WIMBORNE. Lionel . . . Look . . . (*Points to the showcase dummy.* ROACH *turns slowly* U. C., *looks at dummy, stares as though at his own dead body.*)

ROACH. (*Crosses to dummy.*) No! No! (*Tears jacket from himself, throws it away, covers eyes.*) Oh God! I saw him! (*Stares at* WIMBORNE.) Alastair, I saw him! (*Breaks to* WIMBORNE. WIMBORNE *moves* C. *to join* ROACH. ROACH *crosses to witness chair, sinks in it.*) . . . It was me.

WIMBORNE. You've been like a man possessed. It's as though there were two of you.

ROACH. Oh, God, it was me.

WIMBORNE. Lionel . . . You've done too much dam-

ACT III   CONDUCT UNBECOMING

age—I can no longer protect you. . . . Do you understand? (*Draws his gun. Long pause.* ROACH *looks at gun.*)

ROACH. I understand.

WIMBORNE. (*Pause.*) I'm sorry.

ROACH. You will tell the Colonel that—Captain Scarlett—is dead. (WIMBORNE *goes, arch* L. ROACH *swivels on* L. *knee by chair, facing* U. *and shoots gun.*)

CURTAIN

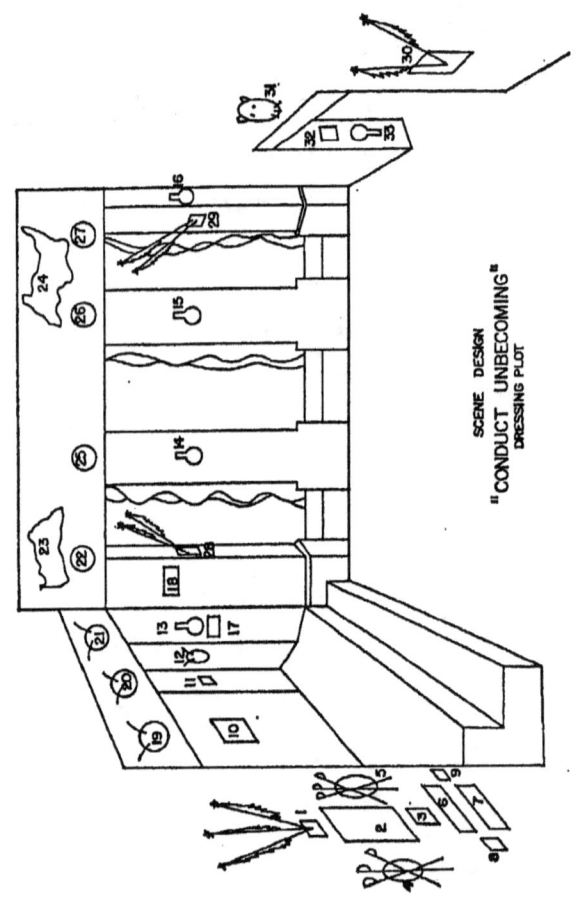

DRESSING PLOT

The numbers below refer to diagram on Page 134.
1. Flag holder with three colours.
2. Portrait of Colonel Millington.
3. Plaque reading "General Sir William Millington V.C. Colonel of the Regiment, 1875-1881."

4 and 5. Sword trophies. Three swords on each.
6 and 7. Photographs of the Regiment.
8 and 9. Prints of various military actions in India.
10. Portrait of a past colonel.
11. Photograph of a "gunners" team.
12. Curved horns on plaque.
13, 14, 15, and 16. Oil lamps.
17. Photograph of a mounted company.
18. Photograph of the Regiment.
19. Antelope head with twisting horns.
20. Boar's head.
21. Antelope head with curved horns.
22. Antelope head with small horns.
23. Animal skin.
24. Animal skin.
25. Spotted antelope with twisting horns.
26. Small antelope with twisting horns.
27. Antelope with short straight horns.
28. Flag holder with two colours.
29. Flag holder with two colours.
30. Flag holder with two colours.
31. Bear's head.
32. Photograph of the Regiment camping.
33. Alligator's head forming small shelf.

N.B.—Curtains (not practical) at the L. side of each arch on rods.

Various creepers and vines clinging to the veranda rail and pillars.

PROPERTY RUNNING PLOT

ACT ONE, *Scenes 1–2*
  SET:
    Black tray and ashtray on table 11, D. R. C.
  STRIKE:
    Polo mallet and helmet from cabinet 10, D. R.
    Gong 18 and hammer from table 13.

ACT ONE, *Scenes 2–3*
  SET:
    Empty decanter on U. end of table 13, D. L.
  STRIKE:
    Two full decanters from table 13, D. L.
    Tray and glasses from table 11, D. R. C.
    Sword and glasses from cabinet 10, D. R.
  RESET:
    All chairs to opening marks.

ACT ONE, *Scenes 3–4*
  SET:
    Three lanterns in arches on veranda and candelabra on table 13 (D. end of table).
  STRIKE:
    Upright chair 2.
    Glass from table 11.

1st INTERVAL
  SET:
    Prosecution table in place of cabinet 10.
    Reset all chairs and tables on opening marks.
    1 chair on rostrum by double doors.
    1 chair L. of table 12.
    Playing cards on table 12.
    Coffee cup and saucer on table 11.
    Book of poems on table 11.
  STRIKE:
    Cabinet 10.
    All glasses, trays and decanters.
    Candelabra and lanterns.
    Table 14.
    Riding crop, cigar box and ashtray from table 12.
  N.B.—Candelabra now placed on Table 17, as dressing for remainder of play.

ACT TWO, *Scenes 1–2*
  SET:
    Court table with 1 carver U., centre of the table and 4 uprights (two either side of the carver).

PROPERTY RUNNING PLOT

Green baize cloths on tables 10 and 13.
2 upright chairs to defense table 13 (one behind it and one u. of it).
1 upright to behind prosecution table.
Colonel's chair 9 to witness position.

STRIKE:
  Table 12 to Offstage L.
  Table 11 to Offstage R.

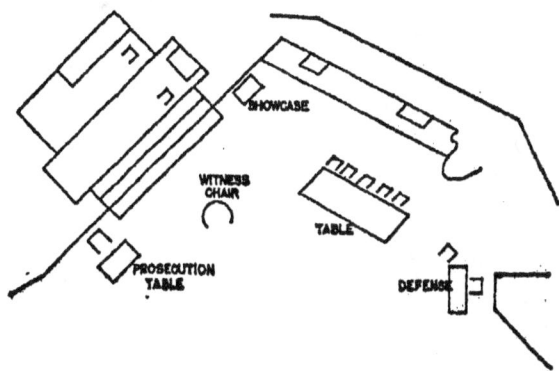

N.B.—Diagram shows furniture positions for Act Two, Scene 2 until the strike of the Court in Act Three, Scene 2. There is no actual prop change between Act 2, Scenes 2–3.

2ND INTERVAL
  Reset and tidy all chairs.
  Pin cloth on table 13.
  Tidy court table, pads, pencils, etc.
  Close up carafes on court table.

ACT THREE, *Scenes 1–2*
  SET:
    2 uprights by arch U. L.
    Folded dress under table 13.
    Carver D. of prosecution table D. R.
    Black notebooks on court table in front of Hart.
  RESET:
    Prosecution table and chair U. to Act Three, Scene 2 marks.
    Witness chair to Act Three, Scene 2 marks.

PROPERTY SETTING PLOT

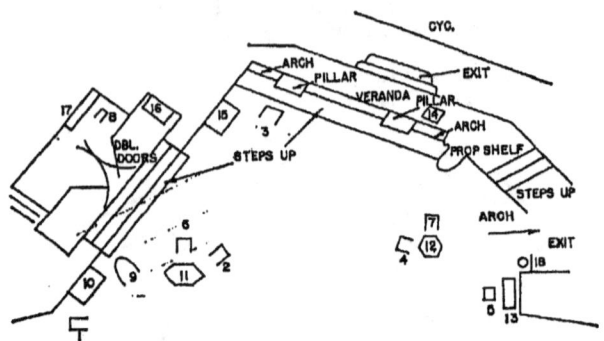

1. Upright chair.
2. Upright chair.
3. Upright chair.
4. Upright chair.
5. Upright chair.
6. Carver.
7. Carver.
8. Carver.
9. Colonel's leather armchair.
10. Glass case with medals.
11. Indian coffee table.
12. Indian coffee table.
13. Occasional table.
14. Occasional table with drop leaves.
15. Display cabinet.
16. Indian wardrobe.
17. Hall table.
18. Gong on wall.

PRESET ON STAGE:
On table 13:
  Oval silver tray with handles.
  1 whiskey, 1 brandy decanter.
  1 carafe water.
  3 brandy glasses, 1 whiskey glass.

PROPERTY SETTING PLOT

On table 12:
   1 wooden cigar box, containing 3 cigars and matches.
   1 glass ashtray.

On table 14:
   Small oval silver tray with 1 whiskey glass.
   Small round silver tray with 2 brandy glasses.
   Square decanter.

Display cabinet 15:
   Workroom dummy with torn, bloodstained jacket. Four medals on jacket.
   Ceremonial sword and helmet.
   White gloves.

Shelf behind pillar U. L.:
   Large round tray with 4 whiskey glasses.
   Medium round tray with 3 whiskey glasses.
   3 whiskey glasses.
   1 red leather cigar box, with 3 cigars and matches.
   N.B.—All these glasses are poured ready for the Mess Night.

PRESET OFF L.:
  The Court Table:
    Green baize cloth
    Blotter, inside large paper on L. and small paper and 1 charge sheet on R.
    Inkstand
    Two carafes and glasses
    1 charge sheet (Hart)
    5 pads and pencils
    Green baize cloth (folded) for Defence table

  Prop table:
    Large oval tray with handles with 7 champagne glasses and 1 brandy glass. 1 brandy decanter
    1 bottle champagne
    1 pack playing cards
    4 black notebooks (large)
    2 black notebooks (small)
    1 empty decanter
    1 riding crop
    1 patrol sword (Fothergill)
    Oblong tray with 5 champagne glasses
    2 upright chairs.

PROPERTY SETTING PLOT

PRESET OFF R.:
  2 pith helmets (Millington and Drake)
  Stuffed boar on wheels (for chase)
  8 swords (for chase)
  3 polo helmets (Wimborne, Hart, Adjutant)
  1 polo mallet (Wimborne)
  1 riding crop (Adjutant)
  1 parasol (Boulton for crow business)
  Candelabra (Waiter 3)
  3 lanterns (Waiters 1, 2, 4)
  3 carrying rods (for lanterns)
  Black tray with ashtray (Waiter 4 for Act One, Scene 2)
  Hurricane lamp (Hart)
  Book of poems (Set in 1st Interval)
  Coffee cup and saucer (Set in 1st Interval)
  3 upright chairs (Set in 1st Interval)
  Wimborne—table lamp (Act 3)
  Standby gun (for Stage Manager)
  Resin box (for actors)
  Prosecution table (set in 1st Interval)
  (exchange with medal case)
  4 piles papers:

  Act One—
    8–10 sets of depositions and 1 pencil.

  Act Two—
    5 sheets of large paper 13" x 8".
    1 charge sheet.
    1 small sheet paper 10" x 8".
    1 pencil.

  Act Three—
    5 sheets large paper 13" x 8".
    1 pencil.

  Act Four—
    6 sheets small paper 10" x 8".
    1 pencil.

N.B.—In 1st Interval wrap Mrs. Hasseltine's torn dress in tissue, tie and mark position of shoulders for Drake's entrance in Act Three, Scene 1.
  Spare items kept in Prompt corner:
    Tissue.
    Wool for dress parcel.

Marking tape for dress parcel.
Cigars.
Matches.
Cigar cutter.
Penknife.

PERSONAL PROPS:

MILLINGTON:
Letter from Colonel.
Box of matches.

ROACH:
Box of matches.
1 cigar.

FOTHERGILL:
1 swagger stick.

ADJUTANT:
1 swagger stick.

WIMBOURNE:
1 gun and 6 rounds .45 blank.

COSTUME PLOT

2ND LIEUTENANT ARTHUR DRAKE:
  1 pair khaki breeches.
  1 red patrol tunic.
  1 pair braces (suspenders).
  1 pair brown riding boots and spurs.
  1 Sam Browne belt and cross strap.
  1 khaki Wolsey helmet.
  1 pair black overalls (trousers) with red stripe.
  1 red mess jacket trimmed blue and gold.
  1 red mess waistcoat trimmed blue and gold.
  1 pair white gloves.
  1 pair black S.S. boots with spurs.

2ND LIEUTENANT EDWARD MILLINGTON:
  1 pair khaki breeches.
  1 red patrol tunic.
  1 pair braces.
  1 pair brown riding boots and spurs.
  1 Sam Browne belt and cross strap.
  1 khaki Wolsey helmet.
  1 pair black overalls with red stripe.
  1 red mess jacket trimmed blue and gold.
  1 red mess waistcoat trimmed blue and gold.
  1 pair white gloves.
  1 pair black S.S. boots with spurs.

COLONEL BEN STRANG:
  1 pair khaki breeches.
  1 red patrol tunic with 5 medal ribbons.
  1 Sam Browne belt with cross strap.
  1 pair braces.
  1 pair brown riding boots with spurs.
  1 pair black overalls with red stripe.
  1 red mess jacket trimmed blue and gold with 5 miniature medals.
  1 red mess waistcoat.
  1 full dress red tunic trimmed blue and gold.
  1 set of 5 full dress medals.
  1 red and gold aigulette.
  1 pair white gloves.

COSTUME PLOT

  1 dress sword belt and sling.
  1 pair black S.S. boots and spurs.

MAJOR LIONEL ROACH:
  1 pair khaki breeches.
  1 white shirt.
  1 red patrol tunic with 3 medal ribbons.
  1 Sam Browne belt with cross strap and pistol holster.
  1 pair braces.
  1 pair brown riding boots and spurs.
  1 pair black overalls with red stripe.
  1 red mess jacket trimmed blue and gold.
  1 red mess waistcoat trimmed blue and gold.
  1 set of three miniature medals.
  1 pair black S.S. boots with spurs.

LIEUTENANT COLONEL MAURICE PRATT (Doctor):
  1 pair black overalls with red stripe.
  1 full dress black tunic trimmed velvet and gold.
  1 set of 3 full dress medals.
  1 pair braces.
  1 black mess jacket trimmed velvet and gold.
  1 black mess waistcoat.
  1 set of 3 miniature medals.
  1 black and gold dress belt and sword sling.
  1 pair white gloves.
  1 pair black S.S. boots with spurs.

MAJOR ALASTAIR WIMBORNE, V.C.:
  1 pair white polo breeches.
  2 pink polo shirts.
  1 white polo scarf.
  1 white polo helmet.
  1 pair brown riding boots with spurs.
  1 pair black overalls with red stripe.
  1 red mess jacket trimmed blue and gold.
  1 red mess waistcoat.
  1 set of 3 miniature medals.
  1 pair braces.
  1 full dress red tunic trimmed blue and gold.
  1 set of 3 full dress medals.
  1 gold and red aigulette.
  1 pair white gloves.
  1 pair black S.S. boots with spurs.
  1 dress sword belt and sling.

1 Sam Browne belt with cross strap and pistol holster.
1 red patrol tunic with 3 medal ribbons.
1 pair khaki breeches.

CAPTAIN RUPERT HARPER—ADJUTANT:
1 pair white polo breeches.
2 pink polo shirts.
1 white polo scarf.
1 white polo helmet.
1 pair brown riding boots with spurs.
1 pair black overalls with red stripe.
1 red mess jacket trimmed blue and gold.
1 red mess waistcoat trimmed blue and gold.
1 set of 2 miniature medals.
1 pair braces.
1 full dress red tunic trimmed blue and gold.
1 set of 2 full dress medals.
1 gold and red aigulette.
1 pair black S.S. boots with spurs.
1 dress sword belt and sling.
1 pair white gloves.

1ST LIEUTENANT FRANK HUTTON:
1 pair white polo breeches.
2 pink polo shirts.
1 white polo scarf.
1 white polo helmet.
1 pair brown riding boots with spurs.
2 pairs black overalls with stripes.
1 pair braces.
1 red mess jacket trimmed blue and gold.
1 miniature medal.
1 mess waistcoat, red trimmed blue and gold.
1 pair black S.S. boots with spurs.

LIEUTENANT FRANK HART:
1 pair khaki breeches.
1 red patrol tunic.
1 pair braces.
1 red mess jacket trimmed blue and gold.
1 red mess waistcoat trimmed blue and gold.
1 pair brown riding boots with spurs.
1 Sam Browne belt with cross strap and sword sling.
1 pair white gloves.
1 pair black S.S. boots with spurs.

COSTUME PLOT

LIEUTENANT JOHN TRULY:
  1 pair black overalls with red stripe.
  1 pair braces.
  1 red mess jacket trimmed blue and gold.
  1 red mess waistcoat trimmed blue and gold.
  1 pair black S.S. boots and spurs.

LIEUTENANT RICHARD FOTHERGILL—SENIOR SUBALTERN:
  1 pair khaki breeches.
  1 patrol tunic (red).
  1 Sam Browne belt with cross strap.
  1 pair brown riding boots with spurs.
  1 pair black overalls with red stripe.
  1 red mess jacket trimmed blue and gold.
  1 red mess waistcoat.
  1 pair braces.
  1 pair white gloves.
  1 pair black S.S. boots with spurs.

2ND LIEUTENANT EDWARD WINTERS:
  1 pair khaki breeches.
  1 red patrol tunic.
  1 Sam Browne belt with cross strap.
  1 pair brown riding boots with spurs.
  1 pair black overalls with red stripe.
  1 red mess jacket trimmed blue and gold.
  1 red mess waistcoat trimmed blue and gold.
  1 pair black S.S. boots with spurs.
  1 pair braces.
  1 pair white gloves.

2ND LIEUTENANT SIMON BOULTON:
  1 pair khaki breeches.
  1 red patrol tunic.
  1 Sam Browne belt with cross strap.
  1 pair brown riding boots with spurs.
  1 pair black overalls with red stripe.
  1 red mess jacket trimmed blue and gold.
  1 red mess waistcoat trimmed blue and gold.
  1 pair black S.S. boots with spurs.
  1 pair braces.
  1 pair white gloves.
     (NOTE: All above uniform tunics and jackets have proper insignia of rank on shoulders (pips and crowns).

PRADAH SINGH:
- 1 white tunic with medal.
- 1 pair black trousers.
- 1 turban.
- 1 blue and silver sash.
- 1 pair black riding boots.
- 1 pair white gloves.
- 1 brown leather belt.
- 1 gold sash.

4 MESS WAITERS:
- 4 white tunics.
- 4 pairs white trousers.
- 4 white sashes.
- 4 pairs sandals.
- 4 white turbans.
- 4 pairs white gloves.

LAL:
- 1 brown cotton skirt.
- 1 fawn and brown sari.
- 1 fawn blouse.
- 1 pair sandals.

MRS. MARJORIE HASSELTINE:
- 1 orange and cream day dress.
- 1 straw hat trimmed with flowers and net.
- 1 cream parasol.
- 1 pair cream gloves.
- 1 orange bag.
- 1 navy walking suit.
- 1 handbag.
- 1 pair navy gloves.
- 1 green silk evening dress trimmed in lace.
- 1 tattered silk evening dress trimmed in lace (exactly the same as above except broken down, torn, and bloodstained).
- 1 petticoat.
- 1 bustle pad.

MEM STRANG:
- 1 lilac day dress.
- 1 straw and lilac hat.
- 1 lilac parasol.
- 1 pair cream kid gloves.
- 1 red and black ball dress.

COSTUME PLOT

    1 pair long gloves.
    1 petticoat and pad.

MRS. BANDANAI:
    Pink and gold Indian dress.
    Sari to match.
    1 pair white sandals.

FIRST CROW:
    1 petticoat.
    1 bustle pad.
    1 pair long gloves.
    1 yellow ball dress trimmed with roses.
    1 gold organza stole.
    1 pair beige shoes.
    1 pair beige stockings.

SECOND CROW:
    1 petticoat.
    1 bustle pad.
    1 pair long gloves.
    1 white spot voile dress trimmed in pink.
    1 white spot voile stole.
    1 pair white shoes.
    1 pair white stockings.

THIRD CROW:
    1 petticoat.
    1 bustle pad.
    1 pair long gloves.
    1 cream wool stole.
    1 brown beige lace dress.
    1 pair beige shoes.
    1 pair beige stockings.

CAPTAIN SCARLETT (Props in Showcase)
    1 old tattered red tunic (to fit Major Roach).
    1 white Wolsey helmet.
    1 pair white gloves.
    1 pair old brown riding boots.
    1 dress sword belt and sling.
    1 gold aigulette.

WAITERS' MOVES AND BUSINESS

ACT ONE, Scene 1

CUE 1:
"The Colonel is just arriving, with the ladies"—Pradah. On clap.
Waiters 1, 2 and 3 run on from D. L. behind pillars and onto veranda.
Waiter 1 stands C. and directs other two where to go.
Waiter 2 stands behind arch L.
Waiter 3 stands behind arch R.

CUE 2:
"We'll go straight out onto the veranda, Pradah Singh"—Colonel. Pradah claps and nods head at
Waiter 1 who makes big gesture with both hands, directing other waiters.
Waiters 2 and 3 run off L. (down steps U. L.).
Waiter 1 follows.

ACT ONE, Scene 2

CUE 3:
During blackout
Waiter 4 sets black tray and ashtray on coffee table D. R. C. Strikes polo stick and helmet from medal case (Enters and Exits D. R. tormentor gap).

CUE 4:
On clap.
Waiters 1, 2 and 3 run on from U. R. (veranda).
Waiters 2 and 3 stand behind arch U. R.
Waiter 1 goes to drop leaf table U. L. (veranda), pours 2 brandies, takes to table U. L. (veranda), sets 3 whiskey glasses (pre-poured) on same tray from shelf behind flat U. L. and sets tray on table U. L. (veranda), waits.

CUE 5:
Waiter 4 closes main doors after Truly's entrance ("Which way did they go?") then goes round behind cyc to stage L. and waits offstage D. L. for next entrance.

CUE 6:
"Drinks for the Mess"—Doctor.
Waiter 3 stands on bottom step inside U. R. arch. Pradah comes to L. of him and gives swords. Waiter 3 takes swords off U. R. along veranda, hands to prop man, and re-enters to stand top of rostrum in U. R. arch.

Waiter 4 enters from D. L. into D. L. arch, collects swords from Adjutant and Subalterns and exits D. L. Then takes swords round to stage R., going behind cyc. and stows them in sword rack.

CUE 7:
On clap (Pradah—"Very good, Colonel").
Waiter 2 collects tray of 3 glasses (pre-poured) from Waiter 1 off table U. L. (veranda)—passes it to Pradah U. C.

Waiter 1, after passing first tray to 2, collects tray of 3 (pre-poured) glasses from shelf U. L. and serves Doctor, Adjutant and Senior Subaltern in that order, standing L. of them in each case. Having served Adjutant he usually has to wait for Pradah to go upstage before crossing to Senior Subaltern—then returns with tray to table U. L. (veranda).

Waiter 3 crosses upstage of 1 and 2 and collects tray of four glasses from shelf U. L. (after sword business). Goes down to stand R. of U. L. coffee table. Subalterns come up to take glasses downstage of him. Hart, on cue in prompt script, steps upstage to take glass and steps downstage again. Waiter 3 then crosses R. to exit R. doors, closing them after him.

Waiter 2, after giving Pradah tray, collects cigar box from shelf U. L. and returns to U. C. and waits. Exchanges box for tray with Pradah and waits. Pradah returns, puts box and matches on tray. Returns to Waiter 1 and exchanges for empty tray. Waits U. L. C. for next cue.

Waiter 1 strikes tray with box and matches to shelf U. L. and returns to table U. L. (veranda), waits.

CUE 8:
"Sing a song, Colonel"—Millington.
Waiter 2 collects 5 glasses from coffee table U. L. and returns to behind arch U. L.—waits.

WAITERS' MOVES AND BUSINESS

Waiter 3 enters U. R. on veranda, comes to steps in U. R. arch to U. R. of Pradah, gives notepad for Pradah to initial, confers briefly, then returns to stand on veranda behind U. R. arch.

CUE 9:
On Millington's passed-out exit.
Waiter 2 gives tray with 5 glasses to Waiter 1 who exits off L., going behind pillars and leaving tray with glasses on U. L. shelf, re-entering immediately to stand by table U. L.—waits.

CUE 10:
(End of Scene) On clap (N.B. All furniture that is re-set goes on original marks).
Waiter 1—resets armchair C., resets upright chair R. of coffee table U. L.—waits.
Waiter 2—resets upright chair C. Collects tray and glasses from coffee table D. R. C. Collects glasses and sword from medal case—waits.
Waiter 3—resets upright chair (Wimborne) to U. R. pillar.
Waiter 4—enters D. L., sets empty decanter upstage end of table D. L. Resets upright chair in front of table D. L.
N.B.—Senior Subaltern has been using this chair. Waiter 4 turns it to face downstage and places it by downstage end of D. L. table to leave room for waiter to stand by centre of table in Cue 11a.
Resets armchair behind coffee table U. L.
Collects 2 full decanters from table D. L.—waits.
On clap.
ALL EXIT—Waiter 1 exits U. L. steps off veranda —Waiter 2 exits D. R. tormentor. Waiter 3 exits U. R. along veranda—Waiter 4 exits arch L.

CUE 11:
Waiter 3 closes main door after Fothergill's entrance— "Millington—Millington."

CUE 11A:
On cue from D. S. M.
Waiter 1, 2 and 4, carrying 1 lantern each, enter main door, move to veranda, hang lanterns in arches, return and wait for cue on top of steps.
Waiter 3 follows 1, 2 and 4 on with candelabra, crosses to table D. L., places candelabra on D. end of table. As he does this Hart is entering D. L. and crossing upstage

WAITERS' MOVES AND BUSINESS 151

of him to D. R. of him. As soon as candelabra is down waiter picks up tray and empty decanter from table and takes them off D. L. Re-enters immediately with champagne tray and stands by centre of D. L. table. Places tray on table. Places brandy decanter and glass from tray onto D. end of table. Pours one champagne glass and places on upstage onstage corner of table for Winters. Then pours six more glasses on the tray, places champagne bottle on table, picks up tray and turns to face onstage ready for Subalterns to take glasses. Ladies exit above him after he has returned with champagne tray.

CUE 12:

On clap (Pradah—as Crows reach "hand kissing" position L. C.).

Waiters 1, 2 and 4 come downstage.

Waiter 1 comes behind white-dress crow and collects her shawl.

Waiter 2 comes behind blue-and yellow-dress crows and collects their shawls. (Crows have shawls hanging over both their arms, and shrug them off.).

Waiter 4 comes past crows, R. of them, sweeps up upright chair C. and, crossing below D. R. C. coffee table, takes it off R. doors.

Waiter 2 hands his 2 shawls to Pradah, collects glass from coffee table D. R. C., exits D. R. tormentor.

Waiter 1 hands his shawl to Pradah, exits D. R. tormentor, following Waiter 2.

Waiter 4 re-enters double doors R., collects shawls from Pradah at top of steps, exits double doors R.

CUE 12A:

Subalterns return empty glasses to Waiter 3's tray.

Waiter 3 turns to table, puts down tray, picks up the one remaining full glass from it, turns to face onstage for Wimborne to collect glass. When dismissed by Pradah exits D. L.

CUE 13:

"—shall not be long"—Wimborne. On his exit.

Waiter 1 enters D. L. with oblong tray of 5 champagne glasses. Moves to C. Business with Millington. Then U. to Mrs. Hasseltine. Then exits L.

Waiters finished for Act One.

WAITERS' MOVES AND BUSINESS

INTERVAL 1. CHANGE.

ACT TWO

CUE 14:

(Setting the Court).

On Drums Pradah enters R. double doors and crosses D. C.

Waiters 2 and 3 bring on court table D. L. (Waiter 3 leading) and set C.

Waiter 1 enters R. following Pradah, carrying folded tablecloth. Crosses to prosecution table D. R. and places cloth folded on top of it. Standing onstage of table, pulls it out from wall to marks, unfolds cloth and lays it, places chair from D. R. behind table, picks up coffee table D. R. C. and waits.

Waiter 4 enters U. R., moves coffee table U. L. out of way. A few feet to L. sets 2 upright chairs for Hart and Boulton behind court table from R. and behind coffee table U. L. Sets chair that was L. of coffee table for Millington behind defence table D. L. Picks up coffee table U. L. and waits.

Waiter 3 having set court table sets armchair from D. R. C. to behind C. of court table for Adjutant. Sets 2 uprights from C. and U. R. behind court table for Truly and Winters, waits.

Waiter 2 having set court table, takes folded cloth which was brought on on L. end of it and places, folded, on D. L. table. Pulls out D. L. chair to well onstage, then pulls out D. L. table, standing onstage of it. When Waiter 4 has set Millington's chair, sets D. L. table into chair, then sets the chair that he previously moved out to above D. L. table for Drake's chair. Waits.

Pradah sets witness chair.

On clap.

ALL EXIT—Waiter 1 through doors R. with coffee table—Waiter 2 arch L. Waiter 3 U. R.—Waiter 4 arch L. with coffee table.

CUE 14A:

Waiter 3 closes main door after Drake's entrance.

CUE 15:

(Between Act Two, Scenes 2 and 3).

On Blackout.

Waiters 1 and 4 enter D. L. arch, following Pradah, stand either side of court table facing in. On lights up mime placing table. On Pradah's clap—exit D. L.

WAITERS' MOVES AND BUSINESS

CUE 16:
>Waiter 3 closes main door after Drake's entrance. (Scene 3).
>Waiters finished for Act Two.

INTERVAL 2. CHANGE.

ACT THREE

Waiter 4 closes door after Drake's entrance at beginning of act.
Waiter 2 waits off L. to collect dress when thrown off and folds ready for next Cue. Also collects wrapping paper.

ACT THREE, *Scenes 1 and 2*

CUE 17:
>Entrance D. L. as follows: Pradah (with 6 black notebooks).
>Waiter 2.
>Waiter 3 with folded dress.
>Waiter 1 with armchair for Colonel.
>Waiter 4 with 2 upright chairs for Doctor and Roach.
>Waiter 2 masks Waiter 3 and tidies papers on Defence table.
>Waiter 3 sets dress under Defence Table U. end.
>Waiter 1 sets armchair D. R. for Colonel. Sets prosecution table and chair U. (table in line with corner of set).
>Waiter 4 sets 2 uprights in front of pillar U. L. for Roach and Doctor.
>Pradah sets witness chair D. and L. (splitting distance between witness chair and prosecution table. Then puts notebooks on court table in front of Hart. *N.B.* These are not used in scene, or touched. Adjutant picks up on exit. Checks all finished—CLAP—and exits arch L. after Waiters 2, 3, 4. Waiter 1 exits D. R.

CUE 18:
>Strike of court during Act Three, Scene 2.
>"I congratulate you, Mr. Millington."
>Waiters 1, 3 and 4 enter U. R. in that order.
>Waiter 2 enters D. L.
>Waiter 4 throws dress offstage U. L. onto veranda; then collects 2 uprights from behind R. of court table and exits U. R.

WAITERS' MOVES AND BUSINESS

Waiter 1 moves 2 uprights from behind L. of court table to U. L. corner beside Doctor and Roach's chairs with their back legs against the steps, as far L. as possible. Then moves C. carver up to R. of these two chairs. The 3 chairs form a straight line, with the carver no further on than the left of the two centre pillars. Exit U. L.

Waiter 2 moves Doctor's chair offstage slightly then goes to left end of court table and strikes Off L. with Waiter 3.

Waiter 3 to right end of court table, strikes Off L. with Waiter 2.

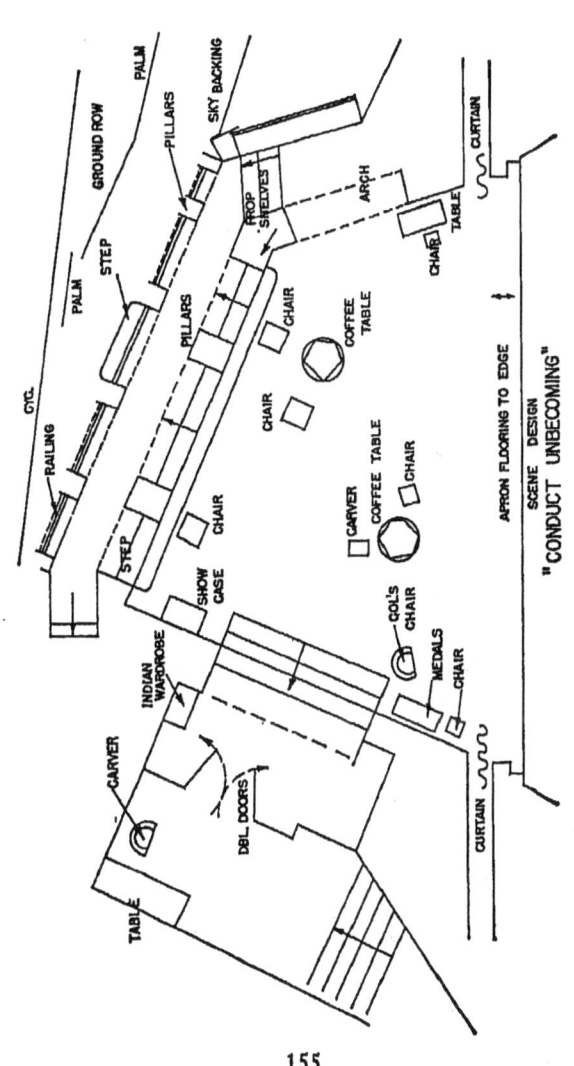

www.ingramcontent.com/pod-product-compliance
Lightning Source LLC
Chambersburg PA
CBHW070643300426
44111CB00013B/2234